the series on school reform

Patricia A. Wasley
University
of Washington

Ann Lieberman
Senior Scholar,
Stanford University

Joseph P. McDonald
New York
University

SERIES EDITORS

(Continued)

the series on school reform, *continued*

IMPROVING
the
ODDS

Developing Powerful Teaching Practice and a Culture of Learning in Urban High Schools

THOMAS DEL PRETE

Foreword by Ann Lieberman

Teachers College, Columbia University
New York and London

Published by Teachers College Press, 1234 Amsterdam Avenue, New York, NY 10027

Copyright © 2010 by Teachers College, Columbia University

Library of Congress Cataloging-in-Publication Data
Del Prete, Thomas.
 Improving the odds: developing powerful teaching practice and a culture of learning in urban high schools / Thomas Del Prete.
        p. cm. — (The series on school reform)
 Includes bibliographical references and index.
 ISBN 978-0-8077-5029-2 (pbk.) —ISBN 978-0-8077-5030-8 (hardcover)
   1. High schools—Massachusetts—Worcester—Case studies. 2. Educational change—Massachusetts—Worcester—Case studies. 3. College-school cooperation—Massachusetts—Worcester—Case studies. 4. Clark University (Worcester, Mass.) I. Title.
        LB 1607.52.M4D45 2010
        373.1100973—dc22   2009026120

ISBN 978-0-8077-5029-2 (paperback)
ISBN 978-0-8077-5030-8 (hardcover)

Printed on acid-free paper
Manufactured in the United States of America

17   16   15   14   13   12   11   10   8   7   6   5   4   3   2   1

For Dad, the first in his family to attend college
and a middle/high school teacher, who introduced me to books;

for Juliana, my favorite reader, writer, and performer;

and for Lena, with whom I learn and live this journey.

Contents

Foreword

SEVERAL YEARS AGO I got a call inviting me to visit the Hiatt Center at Clark University and examine its partnership with several high schools in Worcester, Massachusetts. I had heard of the partnership, but was unprepared for what I saw. Overwhelmed by the authenticity and excitement of the partnership between Clark University and the University Park Campus School (UPCS) and several other schools, I felt as if, for the first time, I saw an almost seamless connection among the teachers in the university, the students in the MAT program, and the teachers in the schools. People seemed to move effortlessly between school and university. Students appeared in the high school as teachers, and also as graduate students in the program. Students were socialized into a way of teaching that was close to practice, rather than the usual suffering of the huge gap between the theory of the university and the practice of teaching in a real school.

I participated in a Round given by a graduate student in the program. There were other students there, and a few teachers–about eight of us in all. The student gave us all a sheet describing the purpose of the lesson, what she had planned, and questions that she wanted answered. I was immediately drawn to this young teacher getting experience in examining what she was doing, asking for feedback and engaging all of us in discussing her work with her students. Rounds, I was told, were an integral part of the MAT and the work of UPCS. The buzz in the air was contagious and thrilling. Here was a school-university partnership that wove together practice, theory, experience, engagement, innovation, knowledge, social change, and shared leadership—all in one place in an urban area with students not expected to succeed. And it appeared to be working for everyone—students and faculty alike. I had many questions: How did this partnership start? What were some of the early structures that began to make the collaboration work? How were students chosen, both in the school and in the Masters program? How did they take to the partnership? What have been the challenges of working in urban secondary schools? And those in the university as well? How have students fared? How do new young teachers do when they start teaching? How has university teaching changed? What structures have helped—or hindered—the partnership? These and many more questions are dealt with in this book.

Tom Del Prete describes in fascinating detail and sensitive prose the life of the partnership, the lives of the teachers and students who participate in it, and the rich context for learning that surrounds them. We get inside classrooms, schools, and community and inside the thinking processes of the students and teachers. We learn their struggles and successes over time in the context of a struggling urban community and what this means for teaching and learning in urban high schools. We also learn about the role of Rounds in helping to build an inquiry stance for teachers, who begin by questioning their own work in a process that helps them to improve, gain insight, and learn. And we, the readers, learn what it will take to honestly improve urban high schools. We are helped along the way by a rich and beautifully written narrative that teaches us how to build a culture of learning that envelops us in some of the central questions of the day—not like in a romantic Hollywood movie, but rather in the authentic struggle to understand high school and university reform. Read on. You are in for an incredible treat!

Ann Lieberman

Acknowledgments

I AM GRATEFUL most of all to the teachers whose practice is represented in these pages: Jody Bird, Ricci Hall, Chad Malone, Chris Rea (a graduate student at the time I was in his classroom), Kate Shepard, Jesse Weeks, and Adelina Zaimi. I have had the privilege of knowing each of them and learning from and with them since the start of their careers; they are terrific collaborators and excellent examples in the profession. I am thankful for the dedicated principals of their schools, past and present: Donna Rodrigues, the irrepressible founding principal of University Park Campus School, and her successor June Eressy, a wonderful teacher in her own right who served simultaneously as principal of Claremont Academy; Maureen Ciccone, past principal of South High, and her successor Maureen Binienda, together with assistant John McFadden. Mike Clifford filled in gaps in my knowledge of the history of the A.L.L. (Accelerated Learning Laboratory) School. There are a host of other teachers at these schools, also valued colleagues, as well as graduate students like Chris Rea, who participate in the professional learning community of the Hiatt Center, and who in different ways contribute to the collaborative effort to develop and understand powerful teaching practice represented in this book.

My colleague and historian Amy Richter also makes an appearance; for her contribution, and for the participation of other Clark faculty members in our school partnership work, I am also grateful. I owe deep gratitude to my colleagues at the Hiatt Center who commit so fully to the work reflected in the book, from whom and with whom I constantly learn. John Ameer, an educator with the soul of a Horace Mann, one of his heroes, provided valuable feedback on the first draft of the manuscript. Ann Lieberman provided thoughtful and timely encouragement and guidance. Others have been instrumental in making the work represented herein possible: superintendents Jim Garvey and Jim Caradonio and members of the Clark University administration, in particular presidents Richard Traina and John Bassett, and David Angel, Nancy Budwig, Jim Collins, Jack Foley, Fred Greenaway, and Andrea Michaels.

I am grateful for the generous financial support that has made possible so much of the work with teachers mentioned above and with their schools. All acknowledgments in this regard must begin with Jacob Hiatt, a Worcester philanthropist who understood deeply and personally the importance of quality education in the life of a diverse community, and whose beneficence led to the establishment of the Jacob Hiatt Center for Urban Education at Clark. Support from the following sources has played a critically important role in the formation of the work at different points during the past dozen years or so: the Arthur Vining Davis Foundations; Bill and Melinda Gates Foundation; Carnegie Corporation of New York; Fletcher Foundation; Bank of America (formerly Fleet Bank); George I. Alden Trust; Greater Worcester Community Foundation (in particular the Greater Worcester Community Scholarship Fund: Ruth and John Adam Founders; and the Norman L. and Dorothy A. Sharfman Fund); Harrington Foundation; Hearst Foundation; Jobs for the Future; Jonathan Starr; Lloyd G. Balfour Foundation, Bank of America, Trustee; Massachusetts Board of Higher Education and the Improving Teacher Quality State Grant Program; Nellie Mae Educational Foundation; Stoddard Charitable Trust; the Woodrow Wilson National Fellowship Foundation; and the federal Title II Teacher Quality and Teacher Recruitment programs.

Finally, I give thanks to Natasha and Andrei and their mom; their patience with my preoccupation and support helped sustain me in the effort.

Introduction

LIFE IS FULL of improbable and inspiring journeys. And sometimes, as we hope, teachers and schools are what make these journeys possible, against great odds. Darius attends the University of Pennsylvania School of Social Policy and Practice. But during his childhood, struggling for orientation as he moved in and out of foster homes, he hardly could have anticipated being there. Nor could he have realized that his entrance into University Park Campus School (UPCS), a small public Grades 7–12 school, newly opened in partnership with Clark University in the Main South area of Worcester, Massachusetts, would become a pivotal moment in his life. But UPCS provided structure, stability, a sense of direction. And he took full advantage of it, graduating at the top of his class and going on to attend Brown University. Each summer during his Brown years he worked in a program housed at Clark to help guide high school students in his home city endeavoring to qualify for college.

Chau, one of Darius's classmates, dreamed of going to college, but became pregnant in her senior year. Notwithstanding, she enrolled full-time in the local community college, but struggled to attain a workable balance between studies—in both nursing and business administration—and caring for her newborn son as a single mom. When her son became sick, she pulled back from nursing, but persisted in earning her 2-year degree. She then turned to Clark, the university she had come to know at UPCS, which promised a tuition-free education to every qualified student from her school. She is a junior at Clark now, motivated by a vision of earning a masters degree, finishing her nursing studies, and opening a nursing home or assisted-living facility in her neighborhood.

Another classmate, Kim, found out that her family had become homeless on the day that she took her first Advanced Placement (AP) test. Nonetheless, she maintained her good standing as a student at UPCS, graduated a year after Darius, and enrolled in Clark. She reflects that her teachers at UPCS "knew me almost as well as my family which really helped them help me succeed" (Surrette, 2007). Kim helps coordinate a mentor program that pairs Clark students with students from her former school and another school in her neighborhood, facilitating relationships meant to strengthen college aspirations. She also teaches at UPCS as a student in the Master of Arts in Teaching program at the university.

Students like Darius, an African American, Chau, an Asian American, and Kim, a White American, are by no means unique at UPCS; in fact, nearly all of the school's graduates have qualified for postsecondary education, and most are the first in their families to do so. Too many of their peers elsewhere, however, cannot count on a school like UPCS to give them opportunity and nurture their hopes and dreams—a school with a powerful culture of learning, fortified by a university partnership that expands its physical, intellectual, and social boundaries as well as its capacity to bring its diverse students together as a single community of learners preparing for college. And so their particular strengths go untapped, their life journeys do not have the same trajectory, and their potential contributions to the larger community are diminished, if not lost.

The stories of Darius, Chau, and Kim raise critical and difficult questions in educational reform, each pressing close upon the others: Why, given the intense effort at reform, particularly over the past decade, does UPCS stand as a rarity, as one of only a few needed beacons in a restless sea? What practices help ensure that students from diverse and economically poor urban neighborhoods, like Main South, develop their academic capability, maintain their effort, aspire to and qualify for postsecondary education, and grow in fulfillment of their humanity? What conditions and challenges have to be met in order to help schools facilitate and sustain this kind of powerful learning for all students?

These questions beg for a discussion grounded in schools and the work of teachers, and they are the motivating force for this book. But they also press on the book, relentlessly and skeptically, their complexity like a stony-faced gatekeeper all too practiced in turning away shallow solutions. And so I address them with due respect and guarded hope, knowing that I cannot answer them fully, yet also with faith in the examples of Darius, Chau, and Kim, their teachers, and teachers like them.

OVERVIEW OF THIS BOOK

I begin, with remarks later in this introduction, by suggesting that the purposes and strategies of reform, as currently constructed, may be too narrowly defined to support the development of more schools like UPCS. Chapter 1 expands this discussion, surveys the perplexities and possibilities of reform, and stresses the importance of refocusing attention on teaching practice and learning cultures. Subsequent chapters explore these themes in Main South, entering UPCS and the neighborhood's two other high schools,

South High and Claremont Academy, to learn from their distinctive histories, challenges, and partnerships with Clark University, and, most important, from the practice of some of their teachers.

Everyone knows or can imagine Main South—a gritty, low-income, urban neighborhood working hard to get back on its feet after a long, steep, postindustrial decline, to make progress toward economic, educational, and environmental vitality, and to keep people, especially young people, constructively engaged and hopeful. The high schools of Main South may seem equally familiar. South High, Grades 9–12, was the first high school in Main South, over a century old. It has had a long history as a comprehensive high school, has seen its population change dramatically as a result of immigration and changing demographics in Main South, and has had to adapt simultaneously to its diversifying population and public mandates under reform. Claremont Academy, Grades 7–12, was originally part of a K–12 school declared "underperforming" by the state after successive years of failure to increase the test scores of all students. Claremont is trying to reestablish its direction as a separate entity after a discouraging series of setbacks. University Park Campus School, Grades 7–12, began as a joint endeavor of the University and the school district. It was conceived as a small neighborhood school with a mission to prepare students for college.

Together these three schools represent a fair breadth of the challenges and opportunities of high school reform, and constitute a revealing comparative group. Each is different in history, culture, and practice, and therefore in how each adapts to and assimilates the demands of reform; yet all serve a similar population from the same area of the city. Chapter 2 reviews the history of each school and how the past shapes the institutional context for learning and change in each one. We enter directly their educational worlds in the chapters that follow, by way of several teachers and their classrooms. Chapter 3 introduces the teachers and the professional concepts and learning practices they share with Clark University, their largest institutional neighbor in Main South and a partner—although to a different extent with each school—in teacher development and reform. Three of the teachers are located at UPCS, two at Claremont, and two at South High. In the heart of the book, Chapters 4 through 9, I look closely at representative examples of their teaching and discuss their practice in terms of curriculum and learning, the opportunity and support afforded students, their level of experience, and their beliefs and ideas. I try to understand as well how their work is enabled or complicated by the sometimes conflicting goals and strategies of reform, their particular school context and culture, and their university partnership. Each moment of teaching thus becomes a window into the complexity and possibility of reform as it gets enacted in particular classrooms and schools.

Concluding the book, Chapter 10 sets in relief the larger lessons for reform suggested by the practices of the Main South teachers who appear in Chapters 4 through 9, the learning cultures of their schools, and the university's role as a partner. My concern throughout is for what purposes are served in the schools, what challenges need to be met, and what possibilities are created or lost there and why. My premise is that an excellent secondary education today will strengthen minds and character; foster an understanding of self, other, and democratic community; nurture hopes and dreams; and prepare students academically for postsecondary education. My main goal is to cast some light on how teachers, and to some extent their schools and a university partnership, can fulfill this idea of education for all students amidst the currents and crosscurrents of educational reform.

THE NATURE OF CURRENT SCHOOL REFORM

There is much we need to learn about teaching and reform in our secondary schools, and about how to apply our learning in particular cases and contexts. Progress in reform is vexingly slow in spite of concentrated efforts. Gaps in achievement and graduation from high school as well as college, in which poor and minority students succeed at much lower rates than their peers, seem to defy intervention, and are gnawing at the national conscience. Nationally, one third of our students fail to qualify for a high school diploma each year, with a disproportionate percentage of these being poor and minority students (Alliance for Excellent Education, n.d.; Orfield & Lee, 2005; U.S. Department of Education, 2006). The gap in graduation rates for students enrolled in college is more alarming; the rate for Black students, for example, is 43% as compared to 63% for White students ("Black student college graduation rates," 2007). If the personal loss is immeasurable, the economic and social costs are staggering, amounting to billions of dollars: The Alliance for Excellent Education (n.d.) estimates that raising the high school graduation rates of Hispanic, African American, and Native American students to the levels of white students by 2020 would add as much as $310 billion to the U.S. economy.

To decisively reduce persistent disparities, to ensure equity in opportunity and achievement in our system of public education, we may need to rethink fundamentally, and not for the first time, our purposes and strategies. In the rhetoric of reform, closing achievement and graduation gaps has been framed rightly as a democratic imperative—as a matter of equality of opportunity and the right and necessity of a quality education if our democratic society is to remain strong and true to its ideals. Frequently, however, this framing is intermixed with another—the need to elevate achievement more generally, particularly in the areas of mathematics, science, and technology, in order to maintain our nation's competitive edge in an increasingly knowledge-driven economy and in the face of a job market defined more and more globally. The distinction between the democratic and economic forms of the argument is significant; the two can be tied effectively together, but often the second framing supersedes the first. The democratic argument focuses us more directly on the plight of schools, neighborhoods, and children where hope and opportunities to learn are curtailed by a host of factors, such as neglect in terms of physical space, curriculum resources, and teacher qualifications. The economic argument tends to fix our attention more on raising content standards and test scores generally than on changing the conditions that create fundamental inequities, thus limiting our strategic vision for reform to a one-size-fits-all approach, although different schools, like those in Main South, might benefit from different approaches, and schools operating under duress clearly need a concentrated infusion of professional and community support.

If how reform is framed shapes the strategic vision, the strategies that are employed in the name of reform have a great bearing on what becomes the field of action for school leaders, curriculum makers, teachers, and students. The No Child Left Behind Act (NCLB), signed into law in 2002, was spurred by both democratic and economic concerns, and brought unprecedented pressure to bear on the effort to ensure that students like Darius, Chau, and Kim stand on the same firm foundation of learning as their peers. But in focusing sharply on testable and quantifiable forms of achievement, NCLB narrowed the conversation about the nature of our purposes and needs as well as the means to fulfill them. If the end is achievement, what do we mean—better test results; greater mastery of mathematics and science; competence in all fields and excellence in at least one; readiness for some form of postsecondary education; inquiring, creative, and morally awake thinkers? If the means are elevating standards and testing, do they meet the goals of achievement and, if so, for whom?

There are broader implications of how we think about and act in closing the gap not only for ourselves and our children, but also for our democratic society as a whole. They are present in ways small and large in every classroom and deserve our close attention as well: What will our education lead us to be and do, individually and together? Will we understand and use our freedom responsibly and act justly? Will we enhance individual opportunity along with achievement, strengthen community and culture along with technological expertise, care better for others and our environment along with ourselves? Moreover, will we take into account our world's need for intercultural understanding, respect for human rights, conflict resolution, power sharing, and greater equity in quality of life? Will we understand the world's growing economic interconnectedness as well as competitiveness, its common as well as corporate, regional, and nation-based interests? As much as we need to diminish the achievement gap, presuming that our social values of equality and opportunity and the challenges of increasing global economic competitiveness are sufficient as rationale, we also need to keep asking the more fundamental question of "What for?" and consider whether our goals and strategies for change, and the curricular and teaching priorities they support, measure up to a vision that embraces a more equitable and sustainable society not only at home but in the world at large.

Darius, Chau, and Kim are symbolic in this respect as well. They represent the remarkable strengths, fortitude, and potential of students, regardless of difficult backgrounds. They also represent moral and social commitment, as they have chosen to apply their education in a professional form of service. They aim to do their part to strengthen the social fabric of families and neighborhoods, the social fabric of opportunity, equity, and community. In educational terms, they have learned how to read, write, think, speak, and act well, and orient their learned capabilities and personal goals with social awareness and responsibility. They are learning not only to stand on their own feet, but to stand for others at the same time.

As one of the university faculty members working closely with their school, as well as with Claremont Academy and South High, I have a privileged vantage point in the effort to learn about reform, teaching practice, and learning opportunities from Main South. I have known the seven teachers who appear in the book for their entire careers, which range from 1 to 11 years. And I have endeavored to support change and the development of teaching practice and learning opportunities in their schools. The teachers themselves all collaborate in various ways in the professional learning and partnership activity sponsored by the Jacob Hiatt Center for Urban Education at Clark University. Indeed, our interconnectedness and common efforts are an important part of the story. For there remains urgent need, and we all must work together to ensure that Darius, Chau, and Kim do not stand alone.

CHAPTER 1

Framing Reform

DIFFICULTY IN MEETING the goal of equitable opportunity and achievement in education, in particularly in our impoverished urban neighborhoods, reflects in part the magnitude of our democratic ambition and the social complexity of the task. Reaching this goal means that we must remake an institutional system in which resources are not equitably distributed. More fundamentally, to ensure a common high level of academic proficiency or, further, to prepare students for postsecondary education and a valued role in a knowledge economy as well as in their communities means changing a deeply rooted institutional culture. This culture, which prevailed in our high schools for most of the previous century, prescribed different academic and vocational paths for different students and expected different levels of achievement. Indeed, many of our recent and current high school teachers and administrators were educated in comprehensive high schools structured according to the belief, proclaimed proudly at mid-century by Harvard president James Conant (1959), that providing different educational paths for different students, beyond a common program of general studies, was a quintessentially democratic improvement of education, as it ensured that all students would have a place at an educational table reserved otherwise for a relative few. That people would sit at very different places at this elongated table, with different consequences for their education, was not a major concern. In Conant's view the advancement of democratic opportunity and equality meant making room for more students than ever before by creating tracks matched to perceived capabilities and aspirations. Democratizing schools did not mean expanding their capacity to educate all students to high levels or to make postsecondary education or work in a knowledge economy within the reach of all; in fact, only a small proportion of students were expected to travel the narrow path from high school to college.

Thus, educational reform today means changing entrenched expectations, belief systems, and structures as much as teaching practice and the allocation of resources. It means renewing schools based on the conviction that all students can learn, and that we are as responsible for all students as for the children who are dearest to us. And if that institutional challenge were not big enough, we also have to confront the impact of poverty on students' readiness to learn and quality of schooling.[1] Poverty burdens a higher proportion of students in the United States than in 24 other developed countries. A disproportionate number of these students are from minority backgrounds (Berliner, 2006). Income gaps parallel gaps in developmental assets—assets like proper nutrition, health care, and reliable adult attention, which most citizens take for granted and which are necessary if students are to concentrate and work well. They also parallel gaps in school resources and, dishearteningly but not surprisingly, mirror gaps in performance; there are many high-poverty schools, but only a very few of those are high performing; and the gap in average achievement levels between students in higher and lower socioeconomic groups has defied efforts to close it (Rothstein, 2008). In broadest terms, educational reform is at once institutional and social change.

Given reform's dual nature—its institutional and social dimensions—it follows that our strategies for reform must be both school and community-based. Like others, I believe that our best chance for transforming educational opportunity and performance where the need is greatest lies in the extent to which we can combine efforts to enhance family and community well-being with the development of strong schools and school and college readiness programs. Political will that coalesces in neighborhood coalitions, partnerships, and larger civic-minded efforts will help make the differences needed to close gaps on a large scale in the long run.[2] Encouragement for such broad-based effort comes from those who have documented the debilitating impact of poverty. David Berliner (2006), for example, reports that modest increases in the income of the poor, at a rate only slightly less than the per-student cost of the federal Head Start program, correspond to a significant increase in school readiness and performance. As he notes, the combination of economic support and school readiness programs might prove the most effective and economical way to enhance student lives and school achievement, not to mention the well-being of our democratic society overall.[3] Most educators acknowledge the critical importance of meeting the developmental needs of students, and addressing the underlying social and economic conditions that inhibit development. Yet they would as quickly assert that we need to learn and do more in the institutional realm of schools in order to make the experience of Darius, Chau, and Kim more common. There is a pressing need to generate and share knowledge that will turn reform resolve into powerful practices and cultures of learning that ensure that no student's strengths and capabilities are overlooked and no student is underserved.

In public policy discourse, however, the institutional structures and practices of education have been a relatively muted topic. Teaching practice and learning cultures are the most important of these least public aspects of reform. They are not entirely neglected, as prominent initiatives such as small school partnerships forged by the Urban Education Institute at the University of Chicago, or New Visions for Public Schools in New York City, or the "pilot school" program in Boston have learning and quality teaching uppermost in mind; but in the realms of federal, state, and local policy making they are relegated frequently to the second or third tier of priority, with test results and/or budgetary concerns taking precedence.[4] In "A Plea for Strong Practice" Richard Elmore (2003) assails the No Child Left Behind Act, charging that its fixation on testing diverts the attention of educators away from the essential but complex task of defining and building the capacity for high-quality instruction in their schools. Certainly, if reform is to succeed, we need to understand teaching practice and learning cultures that enable all students to learn so that they will qualify for postsecondary education, and how to develop them in the context of high schools designed for a much different purpose. Likewise, we need to understand whether the prevailing imperatives of reform encourage or impede them.

THE LIMITS OF TEST-BASED ACCOUNTABILITY AND BUREAUCRATIC REFORM

In confronting the need for educational reform since midcentury, we have moved forward with intermittent passion and resolve, riding waves of economic and social concern, with the federal government taking an increasingly active role. The Elementary and Secondary Education Act in 1965, a concrete expression of the equal opportunity promised by the Civil Rights Act passed in the previous year, provided supplemental funds for schools with a high percentage of low-income families, and has been funded continuously since then. The No Child Left Behind Act is the latest incarnation of this landmark legislation. The significance of NCLB lies partly in its shift in focus as well as strategy: In focus it has moved from leveling the educational playing field to enforcing more equitable outcomes; in strategy it has gone beyond targeted funding and compensatory education to increased accountability by means of testing. To be sure, other initiatives—for example, to enhance teacher quality, expand preschool education, or institute charter schools as incubators of change—are also promoted at state and federal levels and try to gain traction. But during the era of No Child Left Behind the overriding theory of action has been that we will gain better results by demanding and measuring them, that teachers, schools, and communities will find the necessary means for fulfilling the democratic promise of education in the face of stern accountability.

What if we turn that premise into a question: Do test-based account-ability and measurable standards lead to greater educational opportunity, better teaching, and meaningful achievement? We are right to ask whether faith in testing as a lever of educational change and social progress is well placed. Massachusetts serves as a striking and instructive example of why we should. In 2005 and again in 2007 the state was at the head of the class nationally in performance on the National Assessment of Educational Progress (NAEP), viewed widely as the "nation's report card." At both the fourth- and eighth-grade levels, at least 43% of tested Massachusetts students scored at the proficient standard or higher in each of four tests during these years (Massachusetts Department of Elementary and Secondary Education, 2007). This record seems to vindicate standards-based reform and test-based accountability, two of the pillars of educational reform in Massachusetts. Commenting on the NAEP results in an opinion piece in the *Washington Post* (2008), E. D. Hirsch held up Massachusetts as an example to support his contention that content-based instruction is essential in reform and that the No Child Left Behind Act would succeed if implemented well. But, as Massachusetts educators acknowledged, the actual story was not nearly as straightforward or convincing. The good news was that students in general were scoring on average at a higher level than the majority of their peers nationally. But in cases such as fourth-grade reading involving low-income and African American students, the achievement gap was wider than the national average. And overall the achievement gap and corresponding graduation rates in the state remained static and unyielding.

Findings from a massive multistate study by the Northwest Evaluation Association tell a similar story (McCall, Hauser, Cronin, Kingsbury, & Hauser, 2006). At every level from Grades 3 through 8, students from wealthy schools outperformed students from poor schools, and nonminority students outperformed minority students. Furthermore, nonminority students progressed more rapidly than minority students, leading to the disturbing conclusion that even when their performance improves, minority students are still falling behind. These findings conform to data on the recent performance of 15-year-olds on the international PISA tests of mathematics, science, and literacy, as reported by Berliner (2006). The United States is in the middle of a pack of 27 countries in overall performance in literacy, mathematics and science, but performance by White students ranks much higher: Based on the scores of White students alone, the United States has the third highest score in literacy, fourth highest in science, and seventh highest in mathematics. Performance by African American and Hispanic students, however, ranks third from last. Part of the explanation for this disparity lies in the fact that White students more often are in schools serving a predominately White population; de facto segregation and differential school quality based on race and ethnicity persist in our educational system. But if socioeconomic status is considered, another trend holds steady: children who are poor, regardless of racial or ethnic background, invariably score lower than others.

In Massachusetts, as elsewhere, this story line continues beyond high-school. The statewide testing system culminates in a high-stakes graduation test, the Massachusetts Comprehensive Assessment System known as MCAS. The MCAS is based on specific curriculum standards in English language arts and mathematics. Even so, passing it does not mean that students are ready for postsecondary academic work. According to the state's first school-to-college study, 37% of all 2005 graduates attending a state postsecondary institution (community college, 4-year college, or university) had to take at least one developmental or remedial course in their first semester, adding to the cost of their postsecondary education (students pay for a remedial course like any other, but the courses do not earn credits toward graduation) and increasing the likelihood of their dropping out (Massachusetts Department of Elementary and Secondary Education and Massachusetts Department of Higher Education, 2008).[5] The percentage increases to as high as 70% for students graduating from particular urban high schools in the state, with over half of all African American, Hispanic, and low-income students not meeting readiness standards at their respective 2- or 4-year state colleges. By way of comparison, 7 of the 18 graduates (39%) from University Park Campus School (UPCS) who enrolled in a Massachusetts public postsecondary institution in 2005—most of whom are low-income or minority students—were required to take a developmental course. Recent survey results suggest that approximately 10% of all UPCS alumni—whether attending state or private colleges—have been required to take a remedial course.[6]

The state's school-to-college study did find that students who pass the high school graduation test at the level of "proficient" or above are less likely to need remediation than those who pass at the minimal or "needs improvement" level; so one response to the disappointing news in the report is to push students toward a higher level of performance on the test. But that formula begs the question of how much faith in the test as an instrument for cultivating students' learning capabilities and academic readiness for post-secondary education is warranted. As I will illustrate in several chapters, it is precisely because the goals of their school are broader than the test that Darius, Chau, Kim, and their successors are better prepared than their peers for college.

Test-driven reform is the product of our desire for results and, to some extent, a by-product of unmitigated faith in the measurability of things, including learning, and in scientific and technical solutions to social problems.

But standardized testing itself is problematic for a variety of reasons, not least because of the challenge of capturing and measuring knowledge and academic competence accurately and fairly. Even the Scholastic Aptitude Test (SAT), long a rite of passage for high school students, has lost stature; high school performance is viewed increasingly as a surer sign of college readiness, in particular if it reflects qualities, such as persistence in the face of complexity and challenge, that prove much more important to learning in the long run.[7] In *College Knowledge* (2004) Conley maps out the subject matter knowledge more or less presupposed in first-year college courses, and the curriculum gaps that lie between this knowledge and what many students learn in high school. In a more recent work Conley (2007) goes beyond the question of content knowledge and defines *college readiness* as "the level of preparation a student needs in order to enroll and succeed—without remediation—in a credit-bearing general education course at a postsecondary institution that offers a baccalaureate degree or transfer to a baccalaureate program" (p. 5). Such preparation includes the development of particular habits of mind and work, as well as attitudes and skills such as navigating the admissions process. He highlights the importance of habits of mind—such as analysis, interpretation, precision and accuracy, and problem-solving—in meeting the intellectual demands and expectations of entry-level college courses. To these we might add habits of learning and being such as openness, understanding and taking into account other points of view, respectful and honest inquiry, imagining and creating, integrity, authenticity, relating to others, and, not least, joy in discovery and satisfaction in accomplishment—the qualitative dimensions of education neglected in the narrowing of curriculum and discourse that has occurred in the name of reform.

Can standardized tests measure to any degree the habits of mind and work associated with college readiness, and can the combination of standards and tests lead to learning experiences that cultivate those habits? Habits of mind need time to mature and manifest themselves and usually do so through sustained effort in specific contexts of study, as Conley (2007) contends and as the classrooms of the teachers I describe in later chapters reflect. Standardized tests are ill-suited to assessing them; by nature the tests compress and constrain thinking time, and may stymie students with unfamiliar material. Furthermore, they do not take into account variations in each student's pace of intellectual and academic development. Representative samples of work based on meaningful tasks and collected over time are more likely to portray the development and character of a particular student's thinking. Indeed, tests can make certain habits of mind and work an endangered species in classrooms: They are at risk when teachers and students are consumed by testing and measurable results. In such classrooms reform reaches a state of paradox; it enervates what it intends to enhance, stripping both teacher and curriculum of the power to entice, intrigue, evoke, engage, adapt, and inspire—in other words, to creatively harness minds, hearts, and imaginations to the work of learning. The pace of introducing new concepts and ideas may be artificially accelerated as well, thus diminishing a teacher's potential to attend closely to the developmental needs of different learners, and increasing the likelihood that some will be left behind or will drop out. Faced with tight curriculum and testing regimens, teachers often feel compelled to teach in the most expeditious way what will be tested, with the result that students have to adapt and learn with little sense of connection or meaning.[8] *Education* in its root sense means to draw out, but too often little of what students feel, think, or want to convey gets elicited, reflected upon, analyzed, and refined in a test-driven curriculum; thinking and meaningfulness, too, get left behind. Results-only, test-driven reform invariably reduces education or supplants it with something altogether different.

In addition to the problematic nature of testing as a measure of intellectual preparation for postsecondary education, what else might explain the hollow record in Massachusetts, a state with an aggressive approach to reform launched by its landmark Education Reform Act of 1993? Nationally, the Education Trust, one of our most vigilant guardians of equity in education, focuses on "opportunity" and "funding" gaps. The Education Trust defines the *opportunity gap* principally by the availability of qualified teachers and rigorous courses. It notes, for instance, that high-poverty schools have fewer teachers with a college degree in their subject areas than other schools. Also, these schools often do not require that students take advanced courses in mathematics and the sciences; in other words, they do not plan for postsecondary education or work in a knowledge-based economy. Funding in these schools is likewise skewed. The Education Trust (2006) calculates that the national funding gap—the difference in per student revenue in the highest- and lowest-poverty districts—averages $825; a high school of 1500 students therefore has a gap of $1,237,500. Massachusetts has endeavored to address both these gaps. The state requires prospective teachers to pass a test of content knowledge in their teaching areas, as well as to meet other performance standards, before granting licensure. A statewide equity formula requires that all school districts have the same minimal or "foundation" level of funding, with the result that proportionally more state funds go to low-income districts than to their wealthier neighbors. Still, according to the Education Trust (2006), the state is below average nationally in the percentage of state personal income devoted to elementary and secondary education; funding at the national average level in 2006 would have meant an additional $318 per pupil for education statewide.[9] In February of the following year, the Massachusetts Supreme Court ruled in

Hancock v. Driscoll that the state's efforts to fund education since passage of the Education Reform Act of 1993, though open to question, met its constitutional mandate to provide educational opportunity. The ruling doused hopes for a new infusion of funds to lower income communities. The state's good faith efforts aside, as of 2008 Massachusetts had not conducted a formal assessment of whether the funding that exists is adequate for meeting its mandatory education standards; consequently, the foundation budget had not changed in the 15-year period of reform (Berger & McLynch, 2006). In 2008 the governor's office established the Readiness Finance Commission to evaluate the foundation budget as part of a new phase of reform.

Nevertheless, with its curriculum standards, funding formula, teacher licensure test, and comprehensive student testing program, Massachusetts would have to be awarded relatively high marks for meeting the main criteria hailed by conventional wisdom for bridging the achievement divide. Hence the state's sluggish progress gives ample cause for concern. Some would argue that quality of implementation is at issue, that, for example, more vigorous attention to curriculum standards in the classroom will improve the record. Others would maintain that more is needed—more preschool learning, more learning time, stronger alignment of curriculum with college readiness, more overall support along the entire early childhood–to–college continuum, or more school-based decision making. Still others, following the line of sober reasoning that began with the Coleman Report in 1966, which determined that family background rather than school quality is a strong predictor of achievement particularly in the early years, might contend that the state has run up against the limits of what schools in high-poverty areas can do, that demography is destiny, and therefore that social conditions must change before schools can become more effective (Coleman et al., 1966).

There is truth in all of these perspectives. Certainly we need more analysis of the adequacy of funding as well as the adequacy and implementation of reforms bearing on teacher quality and curriculum. The state is also considering additional programs such as universal preschool education to help ensure all students' school readiness. And there are initiatives to strengthen strategic support along the full educational spectrum, with attention to extending the school day and after-school and summer activity, in an effort to build a robust educational and youth development system. At the same time, one must question whether reform as constructed has taken into account the particular and pressing challenges of students and schools in impoverished areas. The underlying premise that families, teachers, schools, and districts will respond and adapt to reform strategies as necessary, and in particular to the get-tough demands of accountability, overlooks the personal contexts from which students come to school, as well as the extent of need and the complexity of the changes necessary to close gaps in opportunity and achievement. We may not be confronting the limits of what schools and communities can do so much as the limits of test-based accountability and bureaucratic reform.

Beyond more equitable funding, better implementation, and expansion of educational programs, we would do well to reconsider the premises and priorities of reform strategy. Three questions seem essential: First, what actually happens in classrooms and schools in the effort to implement reform staples such as curriculum standards and test-based accountability in different settings—is teaching better, are more students enabled to learn, and is the value of what is learned somehow greater? Second, what do we know about the conditions and practices that lead to achievement in different kinds of settings—what do transformative learning cultures and teaching practice look like and how do they get established? Third, are there more educational, democratic, community-based, and ultimately more effective approaches than the largely top-down bureaucratic models of reform?

Of these three questions I am concerned principally with the first two, as well as additional probing questions that follow from them: What actually happens where reform meets practice—what do teachers think about, try to do, and struggle to overcome in helping all students achieve at a high level? What indeed do opportunity and achievement look like inside the worlds of classrooms and schools for students like Darius, Chau, and Kim, and what enables them? Does the kind of achievement encouraged by the terms of accountability enable students to think, read, write, speak, and act well? Does it prepare them for the possibility for college and active participation in the economic and civic lives of their communities? Does it help them value who they are and what they can contribute in our diverse society and world? Much more basically, does it motivate them—not to mention their teachers—to stay in school? What have we learned about real reform and how to achieve it?

REFOCUSING STRATEGIC THINKING ON TEACHING PRACTICE AND THE CONTEXT FOR LEARNING

The fact is that we are still learning about the imperatives of successful change, what opportunity and support for achievement look like in different classrooms and schools in different socioeconomic settings, and how to enable and enact them. In *Turnaround Leadership* (2006) Michael Fullan acknowledges the well-documented correlation of poverty with low performance. But he also finds hope in active reform interventions in his home city of Toronto, in Great Britain, and elsewhere. In examining successful and promising efforts, he has developed a set of 10 elements for change that meets the goals of reform. While he presents each one as necessary, two stand out in importance: focusing on the "three basics" (literacy, numeracy, and personal well-being) and making action a social process. Learning how to help all students read and write for understanding, and understand the meaning and varied uses of numbers, is a critical piece of the reform puzzle. Collaborative forms of action, through which teachers work constructively together, are necessary in particular to minimize variations in student achievement across classrooms.

Class-to-class variations in achievement are common in schools, but more pronounced in those serving students from lower income families (Fullan, 2006). They signal variations in teaching effectiveness from one classroom to another. One way to address them is to establish school-based professional learning practices through which teachers routinely share, examine, discuss, and develop their teaching practice and their students' learning, within and across their grades and disciplinary areas, with attention to examples with demonstrated effectiveness. Collaboration focused on enabling all students to learn, which builds mutual understanding and a shared repertoire of effective practices, is one of the most powerful catalysts for school-based change, as teaching matters above all. Yet the teaching profession historically has not been built on this principle and, while it has been addressed, recent policy making has not sought to change that pattern. Although the professional literature has encouraged the formation of professional learning communities for a long time, teaching is still too often a private and isolated experience, making retention of teachers, including those who feel its vocational pull strongest, all the more difficult.

Why are questions that bear on teaching and learning and the conditions that enable them—on the classroom and school experience of students like Darius, Chau, and Kim—not more central in reform discussion? There certainly has been significant effort to bring them to the forefront. The National Commission on Teaching and America's Future (NCTAF), for example, issued a report in 1996 emphasizing the centrality of teacher recruitment, preparation, and retention and of quality teaching in any effort to improve student learning. In 2003 a follow-up report stressed the importance of organizing schools and allocating resources for successful teaching and learning, advocating in particular for the establishment of small learning communities that nourish and sustain good teaching as well as student learning. The report recognized the symbiotic relationship between powerful teaching and strong teacher communities dedicated to mutual learning and support.

Although persuasive in their rationale and urgent in tone, the recommendations of the NCTAF have yet to take root. To be sure, to implement

them means confronting challenging political, financial, and institutional issues. But they have been overshadowed also by the dominant discourse and
requirements of standards, accountability, and testing. The energy needed to
run the machinery of accountability demanded by the No Child Left Behind
Act, with little or no compensating resources, saps the energy needed for the
actual work of reform at the school and classroom level; it has a central-
izing and bureaucratizing tendency, thus running counter to the NCTAF's
emphasis on teachers and teaching as the strategic locus of reform. The two
approaches exist in a fundamental tension. More broadly, they appear to
suffer from lack of a unifying theory of action, that is, one that integrates
the development of teaching practice with our best thinking about what
matters most in academic learning and personal growth, and how to support and demonstrate their development over time.

Thus to some extent the question of what teachers and school leaders
do to enable all students to learn is held at arm's length by strategies of
reform that are more competitive than complementary. Making teaching
practice a more prominent theme is also complicated by varying definitions
of *teacher quality* and how to attain it. Much current reform policy tends to
characterize teacher quality more in terms of credentials than what constitutes good teaching practice and how it develops. The No Child Left Behind
Act, for example, defines teacher quality in terms of the subject matter of
a teacher's postsecondary degree, under the presumption that more content
background will result in better instruction and learning. Taking a different
tack, some consider teacher quality in terms of teacher diversity, pointing to
the need for more minority teachers in urban settings as the basis for potentially more culturally aware and ultimately more effective teaching. Others
connect teacher quality to measurable curriculum standards, presuming that
greater clarity about what should be taught and what will be tested will
mean greater certainty that it will be learned. Efforts to refine and promote
research-based strategies—what works based on empirical evidence—move
the idea of teacher quality more into the realm of concrete action and practice, more toward quality teaching.

Content background, teacher diversity, curricular clarity, and research-
based strategies are concepts worthy of discussion in reform, but neither
alone nor together do they capture the meaning of teacher quality or school
quality and how they develop. Together with our achievement gap we have
to fill the gap in our understanding of what quality teaching and learning
look like in different settings, how they develop and get sustained, and when
reform strategies help or hinder the process. This is not a simple task, as
teaching is more complex than implied by one-dimensional formulas for
teacher quality, or a single evidence-based method or strategy. Teaching involves much more than knowing and dispensing content aligned with cur-

riculum standards, and the development of an effective teaching practice is fraught with need and challenge. Teaching is also a highly contextual act. A teacher must take into account the academic as well as personal and social backgrounds of students, in addition to a school's overall learning culture and community setting, all while working to establish a common set of classroom expectations and habits of learning and pursuing curricular goals. And the professional environment—the values and commitments held, the discourse about students and teaching, the strategies for learning together—matters greatly. Not least, it has a profound impact on the growth and retention of new and veteran teachers, as well as on the consistency and culture of learning across classrooms. I address these dimensions of teaching in more depth in the discussion of practice in the next section. In the core chapters of the book I try to uncover and illustrate these layers of a teacher's work; my hope is to expand a needed conversation within the world of practice and between practice and policy, and ground it in actual efforts to enact opportunity and equity, develop good habits of mind and learning, and cultivate meaningful achievement in secondary level classrooms and schools.

LEARNING CULTURES AND TEACHING PRACTICE

Do reform strategies lead to teaching practices that meet the needs of underperforming students, in particular those who languish in poorly supplied and inadequately staffed schools and impoverished communities? What happens when curriculum standards or high-stakes testing is introduced in schools lacking resources, using outdated curriculum materials or computers (perhaps with teachers who have little preparation for teaching), and burdened by low morale? How does reform find a foothold in the face of low student attendance, low expectations, and indifferent practice? What can be done about the undermining beliefs that students who enter school already behind in their learning will inevitably fall further behind, that even if different students learn in different ways, only some can learn, have the desire to learn, will learn?

As educators steeped in reform know, these questions defy simple answers. Many would agree, however, on the importance of understanding learning cultures grounded in values of equality and equity and how they develop. By *learning cultures*, I mean the sum of a school community's beliefs, expectations, values, attitudes, aspirations, and purposes and how they are expressed in its relationships, discourse, daily routines and practices, and activities. In an equitable learning culture students and their teachers respect one another. All students believe they can learn, and at a level they previously might not have imagined for themselves. They believe their ideas are valued and that effort is worthwhile; no one is afraid to try. They trust that learning is important to their lives not only in the moment but in the long run.

In an equitable learning culture teachers make a conscious and collective effort to instill in students a sense of efficacy and purposefulness. They proactively help students accept and support one another, learn to learn from one another, learn to embrace challenge, discuss the significance of what they are doing, aim for benchmarks of academic and personal growth that have been carefully illustrated for them, and value and take pride in accomplishment. Teachers assess and hold students responsible and accountable for their effort, but renounce callous judgments that impose self-fulfilling limits on students' capabilities and potential. Instead, linking arms with Jerome Bruner (1960), they challenge themselves with the belief that "any subject can be taught effectively in some intellectually honest form to any child at any stage of development" (p. 33). They challenge students with humility, intuiting that, in the words of James Agee, "in every child who is born, under no matter what circumstances, and of no matter what parents, the potentiality of the human race is born again" (Agee & Evans, 1966, p. 263).

The conversation and learning that occur between teachers as well as in daily teaching practice reflect these cultural characteristics. Once this learning culture is established, students receive a powerful coherent message about how to act and think about themselves as learners. This message stays with students across the variations in teaching practice that they may encounter from one class to another, which otherwise might limit opportunities for learning; a coherent culture draws in all students and draws out their best efforts throughout the school day. Darius, Chau, and Kim's school, formed culturally from its founding conviction and the conviction of its university partner that all students can qualify for college, has these characteristics; the classrooms of the UPCS teachers who appear later in this volume reflect them. As one student aptly put it, "At UPCS, it's cool to be smart."

Attaining a state of coherence and equity in a school's learning culture—that point at which teachers consistently enact powerful beliefs, values, and purposes for all students—can confound the most sincere and diligent effort. To attain and maintain it seems to require that teachers not only unite in purpose, belief, and commitment to effective practice, with routine collaborative ways of acting on and assessing that commitment, but also know their students well and find ways to express their faith in them in their teaching. *Personalization*—an explicit practice of understanding and supporting each student as necessary, of ensuring equal status and opportunity within each classroom and the school community as a whole—is what enacts equity. Personalization, as Kim's words in the introduction suggest, is one of the cornerstones of the UPCS learning culture. Teachers and staff routinely discuss the progress of students at weekly meetings, drawing on each other's knowledge from student and parental communication about family background and the social life of students in the neighborhood, as well as on each other's observations on school behavior and academic performance. They collectively generate ideas about how to address concerns and regroup to form a new plan of action when one falls short. Lacking a practice of personalization and other characteristics of an equitable learning culture, schools have few spiritual resources with which to build their internal connective tissue; they have little beyond the power of their institutional authority, which can be used for better or worse, to hold them together. They will be hard-pressed to develop a community that enables all students to learn.[10]

In schools where hope competes with low morale, low expectations, low student engagement, and tired and benumbed practice, and/or in which behavior control and regimentation take precedence over learning, one of the most difficult things to admit, confront, and transform is the reality of failure. Like other dedicated professionals, and no less than students, teachers and school leaders want to feel a sense of efficacy. And as much as they might value community recognition, they understand and accept the largely intrinsic rewards of their vocation as a source of gratification. Hence student disengagement and poor performance carry considerable psychic weight, leading to self-questioning, if not a debilitating sense of professional powerlessness and failure. Rationalization can follow, masking self-disappointment, covering up for frustration, confusion, or vocational doubt—the emotionally draining experiences that contribute to rapid teacher turnover in schools where new teachers and fresh energy are most needed. Absent reliable forms of internal or external support and a constructive and bolstering process of collaborative inquiry and problem solving, the sense of failure will breed defensiveness, self-justification, and resentment toward bureaucratic exhortations and demands for results.

When rationalization congeals in a school environment, powerful self-fulfilling prophecies infect its belief system, practices, and learning culture. Martin Haberman (1991) employs the phrase "pedagogy of poverty" to characterize the consistent patterns of low expectation and mindless and repetitive activity that supplant real teaching and learning in classrooms of underperforming students from impoverished backgrounds. Where such patterns exist, agents of reform may introduce new standards and prescriptions for learning, but not change beliefs and practice. Thus the script for what has to be learned may change, but scripts for how it will be taught will not; and new, higher expectations may be voiced, but the narratives of students' learning and progress may remain the same. Reform has to take into account the internal logic and sociocultural environments of schools and chart a path toward positive and motivating learning cultures and practices. Even as we seek ways to integrate family and community development with school change, to work toward providing all students with the same developmental assets and school resources, we need to attend to and rebuild as necessary the belief systems, cultures, structures, and practices of schools and classrooms. We need to cultivate the internal conditions of reform, developing communities of support and practice for those with a personal and professional stake in the outcomes. Externally imposed goals and demands will land on poor soil if not matched by the internal conviction and know-how that will fortify and empower teachers, students, and families and rewrite the scripts of practice and narratives of school learning, and if not sustained by the belief that stories like those of Darius, Chau, and Kim should and can be the norm.

For purposes of public policy, student test scores might be taken as a sufficient measure of effective practice. Improving test scores might be construed as confirmation of equity and powerful learning cultures. Practice, however, is not so simply defined, as it is concerned with what is entailed in helping students develop as readers, writers, and responsible thinkers, develop habits of mind as well as core subject matter understandings, and perform well over time. And powerful practice takes time to understand and develop: Knowing what it looks like, what makes it powerful, and how to establish and sustain it is a critical question in the day-to-day life of teachers and students. Much of what we will learn from Main South teachers addresses it, but it is important before we meet them in their classrooms to have a working concept of practice.

To start, I would distinguish teaching practice from specific practices. *Specific practices* might refer to activities, methods, or actions meant to support particular learning behaviors; there are prescriptive curricular packages cast in this mold. They do not necessarily represent the whole of practice; a given teacher, for example, might employ a "best practice" one day and be applauded for the effort, but follow contrary scripts on most other days. *Teaching practice,* or simply *practice,* is more encompassing, having both inner and outer dimensions; it folds together beliefs and understandings about content, curriculum, and students' learning and the particular ways of acting on and assessing them from one moment to the next and over time.[11]

Practice therefore involves much more than knowing content; one might know subject matter exceedingly well but have little sense of how to guide others into this understanding. Content knowledge must be joined to *pedagogical knowledge*—the art of facilitating a student's interaction with subject matter so that content understanding develops—an integration Shulman (1986) termed "pedagogical content knowledge" (p. 9). But the idea of *content knowledge* itself must be unpacked. We are habituated to think of content as solid and static, as if composed of concrete blocks of knowledge to be added one onto the other until some testable edifice is constructed. Some curriculum guides—often an exhaustive and head-spinning compendium of what has to be learned—tend to reinforce this notion, even if not intending to do so. In reality, however, content knowledge encases a powerful hidden dynamic: Much has been constructed through a careful, often painstaking, analytical and social process, usually following the particular way of knowing developed historically within each discipline, such as the experimental method in science or comparative document analysis in history. Attendant habits of mind and inquiry—the "discipline" entailed in disciplinary learning—guide the learner on the journey. To join content and pedagogy means to some extent to expose this hidden dynamic, to find there exciting and accessible questions, and to convert them into powerful learning opportunities that form students' intellectual habits. It means engaging students in the disciplined and creative thinking that ultimately helps them to discern the "good" in good ideas and develop them on their own. How a teacher understands content matters as much as what content is known. Horace Mann made much the same point in 1840, emphasizing that teachers should understand the "principles" of knowledge, "should be able to teach *subjects*, not manuals merely" (quoted in Cremin, 1957, p. 45).

But that is not all. A teacher must take into account what learners understand as well—their preconceptions about particular topics, for instance—as well as their strengths, interests, and prior experiences as learners. This *contextual knowledge* is an integral part of practice. And it presupposes an ability to assess what and how students are thinking about something and to determine what individually and collectively they might need to progress in their understanding, with language and cultural backgrounds all relevant to the process. Even as policy tends to overlook context—with little differentiation between schools and their unique settings—practice, to be equitable and effective, must be intent on particularizing and personalizing. Practice is honed at the edges of interaction between a teacher's understandings and each student's engagement with subject matter.

Content and pedagogical understandings combine with contextual or learner knowledge to form three of four critical elements of practice. Teachers need as well the time and tools to reflect and inquire, to sort through these different kinds of knowledge and how they come together to shape each day's activity. *Reflection* and *inquiry* mean examining underlying beliefs and assumptions in relation to actual practice, and actual practice in relation to the goal of enabling all students to learn. They mean examining the impact of pedagogical decisions on each student in the moment, that is, working to understand what is happening at the point of interaction between student and subject matter. But they also mean moving backward and forward, revisiting what has happened at the end of a class or a day or some longer period so as to better understand what next steps are most likely to gain traction in student learning. Practice is at once responsive and proactive, a matter of learning from students as well as leading them onward. To develop one's practice means confronting personal belief and action in relation to what students think and do on a daily basis, taking it all into account and planning accordingly. It is no more a simple straight-forward march through a prescribed curriculum than it is a universal and reproducible set of actions easily transported from one setting to another. It is multidimensional and dynamical.

If the formation of practice depends on a reflective weaving together of content, pedagogical, and contextual knowledge, then it benefits greatly from a reflective professional environment. If teachers regularly share, discuss, and examine their practice, and frame problems in learning in terms of possibilities of teaching, they expand individual effort into collective practice and wisdom, and collective practice and wisdom into energizing and powerful learning cultures for themselves as well as their students.[12] As Perrone (1991) writes, "Schools that have reflective cultures, places where ideas are thought about, where commonplace beliefs are held up to public discussion, are generally inspiring places intellectually and educationally. They are learning communities" (p. 89).[13]

A strong learning culture for teachers thrives on a shared conviction in the basic capability, unique potential, and inner desire and hope of each student and on a shared determination to actualize them in the face of whatever barriers stand in the way. Teachers manifest this mind-set in their agreement on student performance goals and on what progress in attaining them looks like, in the openness and transparency of their practice, in the alignment of curriculum within and across grade levels, and in collaborative learning practices, which include group strategizing to meet the needs of individual students and joint examination of student performance using a combination of anecdotal information, work samples, and available quantitative data. I will return to these and other themes in the following chapters.

Greater evidence of the potency of the culture and strength of the professional community lies in the understandings, commitments, and work of students. Students will have a clear sense of purpose and understand the learning goals in their classes and their school. They will believe in their capability to learn and will be able to point to specific instances in which their teachers challenge, support, and believe in them. They will value and know where to get help. They will be able to point to an adult in the school whom they trust. Most, if not all, will articulate a desire to qualify for postsecondary education.

REFRAMING REFORM

Recent reform has been imbalanced: more about accountability and results than practice, school culture, and school context; more about *teacher* quality than *teaching* quality; more outside-in than inside-out;[14] more bureaucratic, hierarchical, instrumental, quantitative, and impersonal than personal, qualitative, collaborative, and community-based. Some of the essential areas of change—in belief, school culture, and practice—have been presumed malleable to the one-size-fits-all demands of accountability, or simply left unattended, with all of the hopes and frustrations, internal tensions, and contradictions they may contain.

The landscape of reform has to change. A broad reframing would move from our predominately bureaucratic and quantitative approach—with its stress on accountability, measurable learning, testing, and punitive responses—to a more qualitative, more community-grounded, and in this sense more democratic model. Attention and resources would shift decisively to understanding, developing, and sustaining powerful contexts and practices for learning in different school and community settings, thus rebalancing the legitimate regulatory and oversight functions of state and federal governments with neighborhood needs and ownership. Government would support strategic action to build the local capacity for change as well as networks of exchange and cross-fertilization beyond the local. Action would focus on building contexts for learning that merge in-school and out-of-school environments into a seamless system of opportunity and support for young people. Schools would set development of strong, coherent learning cultures and practices for both students and teachers as priorities, with college readiness, and personal and civic responsibility as core goals, and with community partnerships supporting and enhancing the whole. Public, private, faith-based, and community-based organizations would join together to build the context for learning, ensure that schools and neighborhoods provide the developmental assets that all students need to learn, and assess progress using multiple indicators of growth, such as health, employment, recreational and cultural opportunities, family mobility, and—as key indicators of academic effectiveness—high school graduation rates and enrollment and retention rates in 2- and 4-year colleges.

An agenda for reframing reform might include actions in five important areas: institutional culture and practice; teaching quality; educational opportunity and quality; partnerships and networks; and community revitalization.

Institutional Culture and Practice

- Ensure equitable distribution of students, experienced teachers, and resources.
- Make the well-being of students the center of decision making.
- Shift from external, bureaucratic control to support for internal school development. Develop a flexible and facilitative rather than a hierarchical and directive system that functions primarily to provide support for the development of powerful learning communities within schools in accordance with each school's needs, and also to document and assess progress for purposes of accountability.
- Focus on building the capacity of school leaders and teachers to assume more independent responsibility for operational and curricular decision making over time.
- Build leadership capacity to develop equitable and coherent school learning cultures, collaborative professional learning practices, and teaching practices.
- Make mission compatibility, an equitable distribution of experience, and the development of a strong collegial team the basis for staffing schools, rather than seniority.
- Provide school development support teams staffed by experienced educators for schools that need them, developing a careful process for restaffing schools as necessary.
- Build capacity, within and between schools and within and between partnerships, to expand knowledge of practice and school learning cultures and ways of disseminating it.
- Build capacity for in-school and school-community accountability.
- Refocus curriculum and accountability to ensure readiness for postsecondary education, in addition to strengthening minds and character and fostering an understanding of self, others, and democratic community.
- Loosen institutional control and expand the boundaries of schooling—develop the larger school-community context for learning.

Teaching Quality Continuum

- Vigorously recruit new teachers and establish paid yearlong internships for them. Provide incentives for highly capable practitioners to stay in the profession, including opportunities for nonadministrative roles focused on curriculum, collaborative learning, and mentoring.

- Provide extended high-quality preparation that integrates the best of schools and universities. Develop exemplary programs and school sites dedicated to this purpose. Socialize new teachers into a profession that must be collaborative, collegial, and highly effective and rewarding.
- Ensure that teachers are involved in continuous and collaborative learning at their school sites, in partnerships with universities or teacher networks or effective schools within the community that support the development and sharing of practice.

Educational Opportunity and Quality Continuum

- Enhance the pre-K through college-transition educational continuum. Incorporate school readiness and college readiness programs that align with community and state college entrance requirements. Make the transition to college a matter of academic readiness and choice rather than a matter of age and time spent in school; that is, allow students to make the transition before or after the end of their 4th year in high school, depending on their readiness.
- Extend the school day for both academic and enrichment purposes.
- Combine school learning with community-based youth development opportunities. Ensure that students have opportunities for community-based learning, leadership development, and recreation both after school and during the summer.

Partnerships and Networks

- Support the development of school-university partnerships that build a cross-institutional professional learning community, bringing together various kinds of expertise to strengthen teaching and the pre-K through college learning continuum.
- Support the development of broader neighborhood-based partnerships that bring together public, private, faith-based, and community-based organizations to build the community context for learning.
- Establish regional networks dedicated to helping communities with similar characteristics share knowledge and practice and learn from each other.

Community Revitalization

- Make educational reform an integral part of community revitalization.
- Focus on housing, jobs, family and environmental health, access to public transportation, and family-friendly educational, cultural, faith-based, and recreational opportunities.
- Integrate school learning and youth development with community revitalization, providing youth with opportunities to participate, take initiative, and lead neighborhood and community development efforts.

This is a broad and ambitious outline and well beyond the scope of my intent to try to detail. Its significance for my purpose is to show how my focus on the contexts, cultures, and practices of teaching and learning fits into a larger vision of reform. But, even as I write, a vision along these lines is gaining momentum in the state of Massachusetts. The state's new Readiness Project is a comprehensive pre-K through college plan (Patrick Administration Action Agenda, 2008). Among many noteworthy proposals, the plan calls for a statewide child and youth data and reporting system, student support coordinators in low-income schools, and tuition-free access to state community colleges. As promising and exciting as it is, however, this radical departure from a bureaucratic model will only be as effective as the new generation of teaching practices and learning cultures that develop in the different school and community contexts of the state.

The next chapter describes the historical and cultural factors that shape the learning environments at Claremont Academy, South High, and University Park Campus School, setting the stage for the chapters on teaching that follow. Many of the students in these schools come from the same neighborhood; and the teachers whose work I will highlight all have strong connections to the University. These commonalities make the differences in their experiences all the more vivid and instructive.

CHAPTER 2

Constancy and Change in Main South High Schools

CLARK UNIVERSITY and three high schools—Claremont Academy, South High School, and University Park Campus School—are all located in Main South, an ethnically diverse and low-income neighborhood in Worcester, Massachusetts. The state's second largest city, Worcester has about 175,000 residents. Of the more than 23,000 students in the city's public schools, more than 60% are considered low income and a comparable proportion are described as minority (Worcester Public Schools, 2007).

On the north side of the neighborhood, along a congested segment of Main Street, Hispanic, Vietnamese, Albanian, and African shops huddle close together. The Main South high schools, which serve about one fourth of the high school population in the city, reflect this concentration of diversity in their student bodies. Two thirds of their students are considered minority. More than 40% are identified as Hispanic or Latino, with an additional 25% split between African American and Asian American. Well over half the students come from homes in which English is not the primary spoken language; their parents converse in languages originating in Latin America, Southeast Asia, Africa, and Eastern Europe. About three fourths are low income, qualifying for the federal free or reduced-price lunch program (see Table 2.1 for data for each high school). Most do not have parents with college experience. Nevertheless, the percentage of Main South students who say they plan to attend a 2- or 4-year college upon graduation is overall the strongest in the district, with UPCS leading the way, with 100% in most years, and South High on a steady upward trajectory, increasing from 79% to 95% over the past 5 years (Worcester Regional Research Bureau, Inc., 2008).

SOUTH HIGH AND THE CHALLENGE OF CHANGE

The most celebrated graduate of South High School is Robert Goddard, valedictorian of the class of 1904. The university in 1904 was visible from

Table 2.1. Main South High School Demographic Data 2007–08

	Enrollment	White	Hispanic	African American	Asian	Nonnative English speaker	Low income
Claremont Academy	364	27%	51%	9%	11%	61%	82%
South High	1402	32%	40%	16%	12%	53%	72%
UPCS	227	35%	40%	9%	16%	57%	74%

Source: Worcester Public Schools (2007).

South High, barely a block away. In time Goddard would find his way there, earn a PhD in physics, and combine knowledge, imagination, and youthful desire to launch the world's first liquid-fueled rocket. But the neighborhood defined by South High and Clark as Goddard knew it at the turn of the twentieth century would be much different by the turn of the twenty-first.

Goddard attended a stunningly new South High, resting squarely on a massive foundation of granite in anticipation of a long stay in a growing area of the city. Large attractive Victorian houses stood elegantly nearby; over time they would be surrounded by an increasing number of "three-deckers"—three-story dwellings built in Worcester to efficiently house extended families or multiple families. Together with a strong manufacturing base—firms such as the Worcester Corset Company and Knowles Loom Works stretched in an arc of factory buildings and machine shops across the eastern side of Main South toward the railroad tracks—the three-deckers were attracting a new immigrant workforce. Goddard dreamed of the rocket while Irish, French Canadian, and Swedish immigrants, predecessors to Italian and Polish arrivals, dreamed of opportunity, building Worcester's ethnic foundation for the coming century. Main South was entering a period of rapid growth with every indication of vitality.

But by the 1970s the manufacturing base was hollowing out. Business was relocating to the American South to take advantage of cheaper labor, leaving behind a blight of brownfield sites. And many longtime residents, including second- and third-generation immigrant families whose histories in Main South began during Goddard's time, were moving to nearby suburbs. Worcester, like many New England cities, was struggling to get its postindustrial bearings. The city entered a long and trying period of transition, endeavoring by century's end to redefine itself as a service and education center, as well as a contributor in the field of biotechnology, taking advantage of the intellectual capital afforded by its many colleges. In the meantime absentee landlordism crept into Main South, and the Victorians and three-deckers sagged into disrepair. There were other encroachments: crime, prostitution, gang activity, as well as poverty. South High was moved—its old home diagonally across from the university became the Goddard Elementary School of Science and Technology—and the new wave of immigration that would gather surprising force and sweep into Main South schools had begun.

In 1950 the Worcester population was almost entirely—99.2%—White (Worcester Regional Research Bureau, Inc., 2001). Apart from a small number of African Americans, many of whom traced their roots in Worcester to the colonial or antebellum periods, and a time of simmering local antislavery sentiment,[1] the face of the city reflected the impact of European immigration. There was little reason to question the concept of the comprehensive high school that Harvard president James Conant would soon trumpet, with citizens reasonably confident of employment in an expansive postwar economy. Institutions such as Worcester Polytechnic Institute, Clark University, and the College of the Holy Cross, along with one of the state's teacher colleges (now Worcester State College), offered other options. South High was a symbol of continuity and stability.

But by the 1970s South High needed to expand its capacity. It was built anew in a wooded area at the edge of the city, a pastoral site in comparison to its gritty former home. The new South High was a model of economical, open-space design; educational leaders envisioned a learning environment freed from the impediments of walls and closed classrooms, and built on principles of curricular dialogue and collaboration. But the unbounded physical space did not spur the intended transformation in culture and practice. In hindsight, South High lacked sufficient opportunity to ponder and prepare for the possibilities offered by its unfamiliar seamless space; and so it carried much of its old culture and way of being into its new venue. A cacophony of lecture and direct instruction filled the open spaces, along with makeshift room dividers. And so did the changing school population. The end-of-century demographic wave reached its peak soon after the new South opened, in the 1980s and 1990s. The Hispanic population in the city grew fourfold; by 2000 almost one fourth of the population was non-White. By 2003 the minority population in the school district had become the majority, with the proportion reaching two thirds in Main South high schools.

When Robert Goddard attended South High, earning a high school diploma was not the norm, notwithstanding a long tradition of compulsory schooling in Massachusetts through age 14. His graduating class numbered 93 students, 48 of whom planned to attend college. The entire high school population in the city was 10% of the overall school population (Worcester Public Schools, 1905). In 1950, that percentage had risen by 10 points. A century after Goddard's graduation, it had risen by 10 more (Worcester Public Schools, 1951, 2006).[2] At the turn of the twenty-first century a high school diploma was widely acknowledged as the minimal acceptable level of attainment, and increasingly connected to readiness for postsecondary education at a 2- or 4-year college or work in a new economy. The new statewide system of accountability, launched on the heels of the expansive educational reform act passed in 1993, had already recalibrated the meaning of a diploma, linking it to a set of common academic standards and a corresponding testing program, although not with a consensus view of college readiness standards. The meaning of schooling and democratic opportunity had become more egalitarian since midcentury: The expectation was that all students would graduate and meet graduation requirements different from those that might have applied to them in one of the vocational tracks of the traditional comprehensive high school and different from those to which schools like South High had long been accustomed.

Faced with a welter of changes out of its immediate control, South High's main adjustment strategy was to add on where it could and persevere in what had worked before. It accommodated both a growing bilingual program and the largest special needs program at the high school level in the district, then added technology and school-to-work programs and eventually a tutoring program for students who failed the high-stakes state test. But as it approached the end of the century its attendance rate was low, below 90%, and its dropout rate was high, ranging from 7 to 15% depending on how it was calculated (Worcester Regional Research Bureau, Inc., 2003).[3] Reflecting the unstable life of new immigrants and families living in poverty in Main South, it had a disruptive mobility rate, with students coming and going daily, creating fluctuations that subjected its open spaces to unpredictable periods of overcrowding.

South High was at a historical and cultural crossroads. Its additive strategy for accommodating its increasingly diverse student body followed the unspoken but deeply ingrained logic of the comprehensive high school model and its outdated view of equality of opportunity in education: Make more and different educational pathways and programs for different students, based on fundamentally different expectations and projections for their work lives. It tried to hold together its disparate parts, putting different students into different programs and categories of ability, even while confronted with the question of how to educate all students to a high level of common achievement—indeed, with how to keep them in school. It was an untenable position, yet it would take time before South would venture outside its long-familiar cultural lens and consider addition by subtraction: the prospect of enhancing learning by reducing and fundamentally refocusing its programs, mission, culture, and practices. In the mid-1990s the superintendent of Worcester Public Schools considered ways to relieve the pressure on South High. He had a proprietary sense of care for the school because he had been principal there and appreciated firsthand its particular needs. He challenged the university to help by, first of all, considering support for an additional secondary school for Main South students.

UNIVERSITY PARK CAMPUS SCHOOL: REINVENTING HIGH SCHOOL IN PARTNERSHIP

For a long time the presence of Clark University in its immediate neighborhood was as silent and anonymous as the shadow it cast. Families attending the churches along the Main Street corridor bounded on one side by the university, individuals sheltering momentarily at the bus stop facing one of the university's brick facades, or young people hovering about the adjacent convenience store just before or after school would regard the buildings standing stolidly nearby as no more than a familiar visual landmark. Even the city-owned University Park, a block-sized swath of green opposite the university on Main Street, with its duck pond and stalwart beech and maple trees gracing the area since Goddard's youth, did little to draw out the residents of the university. The university maintained an inward focus, keeping the business of developing and sharing knowledge separate from its immediate environment, even as, ironically, it hoped to impact the larger world. There was a simple wrought iron fence cornering one section of campus, but otherwise no walls demarcated the University grounds; yet it was entirely self-enclosed.

As the neighborhood deteriorated, however, with growing evidence of crime, gang activity, and prostitution, the negative impact on the attractiveness and reputation of the university could not be ignored. In the mid-1980s, charged with an enlightened sense of self-interest, Clark University stepped gingerly over its insular boundaries and began to collaborate with community members to revitalize the neighborhood. Within a decade it had assumed the role of proactive and protective partner, forming with the Main South Community Development Corporation, area churches, businesses, residents, and local schools the University Park Partnership (UPP). The efforts of the UPP since that time have been enormously fruitful, resulting in rehabilitated properties, increased ownership of homes by residents, new small businesses, a new $9.2 million Boys and Girls Club (which replaced one built during Goddard's youth), social and educational programs, and an entirely new and mutually transforming relationship between the university and the neighborhood.

While changing its posture as resident outsider to engaged neighbor, the university was awarded a grant on behalf of the UPP from the federal Department of Housing and Urban Development (HUD). The UPP had proposed a comprehensive plan for revitalizing the worn and stagnant neighborhood, which included an outline for a new neighborhood secondary school: University Park Campus School—Darius, Chau, and Kim's school—would test directly the proposition that education can simultaneously change lives and build neighborhood vitality. The idea of the school was promoted by the superintendent of Worcester Public Schools, who viewed it as a way to give new opportunity to students losing ground in crowded South High.

Beginning in 1996 the HUD funds allowed for a yearlong period of incubation for the school at the Jacob Hiatt Center for Urban Education at Clark University. The center had been established several years before through the generosity of Jacob Hiatt, a local, civic-minded businessman, Clark trustee, and graduate alumnus, and fervent advocate of educational opportunity. "We must allow our children and their teachers to dream," he said, "and to have their dreams come true."[4] Hiatt believed in the power of the University to help schools learn to educate diverse students and immigrant children; as an immigrant himself (from Lithuania), he understood firsthand the need and the possibility.

Having just begun a partnership with several Main South schools focused on teacher preparation, professional learning, and exemplary practice, the Hiatt Center was in a good position to support the process of planning the new school. The university as a whole, however, was initially cautious. As fortuitous as it might seem, the convergence of the neighborhood initiative, Jacob Hiatt's philanthropic vision, and the engaged scholarship of the center in the form of a school partnership could not move forward without examination. A university committee comprising administrators and faculty was charged with carefully sorting through the implications of this kind of involvement and the commitments it would entail. The committee raised questions about the impact of the proposed school partnership on faculty and resources, but ultimately did not stand in the way of the idea. If the committee's endorsement was rather reserved, it had no inkling of the influence the school would come to have in the formation of the university's own sense of identity and as a manifestation of its mission of social engagement. In fact, as much as UPCS was born of conviction, resolve, and hope, no one quite foresaw its transformative impact.

Thus, in conjunction with the school district, Clark University became midwife to a new public secondary school dedicated to serving students living in its immediate neighborhood. The targeted area stretched east to west over Main Street, and more than a dozen blocks north to south. The university offered its greatest resource to the approximately 5,000 residents of this area—a tuition-free undergraduate education to those who had lived in the neighborhood for 5 years or more and qualified for admission. This commitment was meant to encourage residential stability and social, economic, and personal growth. It also radically altered the landscape on which students attending the new school could map their futures. The university had swung open its doors and created a new pathway of possibility; however they had begun to imagine their future lives, young students now had a much wider field of opportunity than before.

A joint committee of university and school district personnel framed the policies that guided the development of University Park Campus School and wisely selected as its first principal a neighborhood resident and devoted teacher of Spanish from South High who had worked as a teacher-leader in the Hiatt Center's newly developed collaborative teacher preparation program. Neighborhood residents were informed of the school during a series of open meetings at the university. The first class of students was selected by lottery, a practice that continues; approximately 100 of the 150 neighborhood students eligible each year apply for 35–40 places. The school was launched in the fall of 1997 with a seventh-grade class of 34 students that included Darius and Chau. By design it unfolded slowly, with a new class added each year, allowing the staff, which included Hiatt Center graduate students, to nurture a culture of achievement and college aspiration. By their junior year students were eligible to take a course at the university based on their emerging academic strengths. Because of its mission to prepare all students for postsecondary education and the possibility of attending Clark, UPCS was dubbed the "school with a promise."

Darius, Chau, and their classmates did not cross the threshold of the new school as accomplished students. Their average reading level was barely third grade. Yet, in a pattern that would be repeated by students in succeeding classes, they progressed remarkably. They all passed the new state test required for graduation on their first try as tenth graders in 2001. All but one student since has done the same, the vast majority scoring at the two highest ("proficient" and "advanced") of three passing levels, setting a high standard for urban schools in the state. Darius and 12 of his classmates completed at least one course at Clark University before graduating, again providing a powerful example for upcoming classes. Just as striking and important, all qualified for some form of postsecondary education upon graduation in 2003, whether at a technical school or 2- or 4-year college.

By any measure, the educational attainment of the first UPCS class—the considerable distance each student traveled from seventh grade to graduation—was extraordinary. But the students, their teachers, and their university partner had more to learn about postsecondary readiness. Progress slowed appreciably at the postsecondary level, and a number of students dropped out within a year. While most have since returned to their postsecondary studies, with many, like Chau, on track to graduate from college within 6 years, their false start caused prolonged rethinking about what academic preparation for college means and what nonacademic preparation is necessary. Those of us involved concluded generally that students were academically but not socially ready; they were not prepared for the shift to more independent and self-directed learning, not ready to navigate a more complex and much less structured and protective learning environment. This conclusion was later confirmed through a survey and a series of interviews with alumni.[5]

Accordingly, the senior year at UPCS has been redesigned as a transition-to-college experience, with greater stress on independent reading, writing, and research, and more guidance on college admissions and preparing for college life (explained in more detail in Chapter 10). Students who do not qualify to take a course at Clark University for credit spend at least some time auditing one. Most students have greater familiarity with the Clark campus and college life through a mentor program that pairs university and UPCS students: University mentors meet with UPCS 9th, 10th, and 11th graders on campus for planned activities, and talk about how to be a successful student in college. In addition, UPCS alumni, such as Darius, Chau, and Kim, together with school and university staff meet with current students and parents to reflect on the various dimensions of college preparation and success.

As a consequence of these additional programs and options, the college retention rate of UPCS students has improved markedly. Among the approximately 160 students who have graduated since 2003—nearly all of whom are the first in their families to attend college—at least 140 have graduated from a 2- or 4-year college or are on track to complete a degree, with only 10% required to complete remedial courses along the way. This record far surpasses the norm for low-income students, who attend college at a much lower rate than others, with proportionally fewer, in the range of 6–7%, graduating within 6 years.[6] UPCS has become one of the most accomplished schools in this respect in the country; and it is still learning and improving.[7]

PRECURSOR TO CLAREMONT ACADEMY: THE DEMISE OF A BOLD MODEL

While UPCS was developing as an alternative for Main South students living in the Clark University environs, plans were underway to introduce a new K–12 school to the northern edge of the university campus, which would become, as it turns out, the precursor to Claremont Academy. The school would be a "Co-NECT" school, one of many emerging reform models nationwide. Designated the "Accelerated Learning Laboratory" or "A.L.L.

School," the concept of the school was alluring, with a cutting-edge feel and an unabashed declaration of faith in the power of technology and the pragmatic know-how it implied to induce learning. Promoted by BBN, a firm specializing in technological solutions to problems, the model stressed the use of technology and collaborative, interdisciplinary, and project-based learning. To add relevance and dynamism to the concept, the A.L.L. School adopted a global studies theme, which it would address partly by harnessing the new connective power of the Internet in the curriculum.

Though tantalizing in concept, the curricular design of the school was by no means simple to implement. It required an exceptional degree of interdisciplinary planning, technological know-how, and subject matter expertise. It meant devising new curricular and assessment practices. These were demanding preconditions for success. The challenge of actualizing the school's vision was compounded by its K–12 expanse, and the fact that different grade levels developed at different locations during its crucial formative period, while all awaited completion of the new building located a few blocks from the main Clark campus. In 1999, when all the grades and teachers were finally united, the model struggled to gain traction, facing a steeper and more frictional road than previously imagined. Not least, the A.L.L. School had to adapt to new state curriculum standards just as it was trying to establish its own standards based on the interdisciplinary model. Magnet school funding disappeared within a year, unhinging support for the global studies theme and abruptly stopping the flow of students from different parts of the city. Neighborhood students streamed into the school in their stead, bringing with them a new set of literacy needs not accounted for in the curriculum design. Teachers committed to the original, but now moribund, model left. The first principal retired soon after the school opened its new home, and her successor left the district within a few years. It was hard to maintain a sense of continuity or direction.

Consequently, at the turn of the twenty-first century both South High and the A.L.L. School were culturally adrift, for different reasons. South had to confront its embedded identity as a comprehensive high school and its corresponding additive program strategy for change; the A.L.L. School needed to reconsider its founding vision or establish a new one. Both were pressed to respond to the new, demanding state accountability system. Both had to redefine practice in relation to the literacy needs of its ethnically and linguistically diverse students, increase personalization, and meet new standards of equity. Each had to revisit its mission, and consider how to shift to a culture that supports college readiness, that embraces and elevates all students. Each had to interrogate and rethink the template upon which its school had been designed.

ADVERSITY, OPPORTUNITY, AND PROMISE

Opportunity to set a new course in the histories of the schools came in the form of a systemic high school change initiative spurred by the national Schools for a New Society program sponsored by the Carnegie Corporation of New York in collaboration with the Bill and Melinda Gates Foundation. Worcester school and community leaders, with Clark University acting as the facilitating partner, contemplated how to remake the city's high schools so as to enhance achievement for all students. Many imagined the transformation of the large comprehensive model into sets of small schools, each with a compelling theme to entice student interest, fortified by collaboration with a community partner, each with a robust academic program and new forms of academic support within, across and beyond the core academic curriculum, with an emphasis on literacy and numeracy, and each with new opportunities for student voice and family involvement. Each small school would be dedicated to establishing a new culture based on principles of equity, personalization, literacy development, postsecondary readiness, teacher collaboration, youth development, community partnership, and achievement. Developing a comprehensive school and community plan over a period of fifteen months, the Worcester team of school, university, and community leaders was awarded an implementation grant from Carnegie in fall 2001.[8]

The Development of Small Academies at South High

At South High a ninth-grade team of teachers took the lead in developing a prototype small learning community, the Information Technology Academy (ITA). They built time into the new ninth-grade schedule for teacher planning, student conferencing, and a weekly "student congress." In addition to a technology class, they introduced new literacy and numeracy classes for students needing extra support, with related professional development provided by the Hiatt Center. They defied the conventional comprehensive high school wisdom that sorted students into different vocational or ability groups, not trusting that equity could be served in this model. They challenged themselves instead to hold high expectations for all students and to personalize their teaching by making core academic classes heterogeneous. Students would be encouraged to do extra work to qualify for an honors-level grade. All would be assessed regularly on their progress, using a set of rubrics to make learning goals comprehensible and transparent. Rather than ask students to move from one broad, open, multiclass space to another, a typical travel pattern for South High students, they decided to collect the whole ninth grade into a common space, where all core academic subjects would be addressed in a set of rooms demarcated by dividers, leaving open the possibility of the interdisciplinary collaboration imagined at South many years before. The teachers committed to an inclusive community, a focused culture of learning, and an ethic of equity.

Two other South High academies—Arts and Humanities, and Education, Service, and Government—began a year after the ITA started. Both expanded academic support for low-performing incoming ninth graders to help them gain academic traction in the transition to high school, adding either a literacy or numeracy class or both. Neither one adopted the heterogeneous grouping model of the ITA, although both dropped the last of four levels of student grouping. The remaining three levels of classes—(1) advanced placement, (2) honors, and (3) college—were all intended to support college readiness. Whether a new culture of high expectations and equitable practice could take root across these three levels, however, was and remains a critical question (this question surfaces in the discussion of Jesse Weeks's ninth grade college-level history class in Chapter 9 and a parallel discussion of Claremont teacher Adelina Zaimi's ninth-grade mathematics class in Chapter 5). Both the ITA and UPCS rejected this practice, wary of the legacy of tracking in comprehensive high schools and the power of tracking categories to wrongly predetermine and delimit a student's potential. At UPCS both the floor and ceiling of expectations have been raised, for teachers as well as for students, by designating all courses as honors level beginning in ninth grade, and by providing both advanced placement and university course options for all students as they progress through high school.

The plan for all academies at South High was to grow slowly, one grade at a time. In theory, this incremental approach would allow teachers time to plan successive grades and build the community culture. In other words, it was based on the idea that the tipping point of cultural change more likely would be attained through an evolutionary rather than revolutionary transformative process. But the gradualist approach was as much a sign of cautiousness and guardedness. Although leadership had tried to prepare the way for change, the ITA was leading a countercultural movement up a rugged slope with no clear path to the summit.

The three academies continue at South, but after several years they have not progressed beyond the 9th and 10th grades, and their original vision has eroded with time. It is tempting to cite the tentative pace of change and lack of political unity as the reasons for their stalled development; indeed, some of us involved would contend that a more dramatic and decisive step forward in favor of a more independent academy structure might have yielded more. Yet this view risks oversimplifying the magnitude and complexity of the task of changing the culture and practice of schools like South High, and the lessons it contains.

A host of factors have inhibited progress and threaten the integrity of the academies. From the outset, South High faced strong internal resistance among groups of teachers to what amounted to a seismic historical shift, in spite of a compelling argument for change. It labored without a concerted plan for transforming minds and hearts, and with the school district and wider community, including the university, unable to make their support for change more persuasive for all teachers at the school level. The politics of contractual negotiation interfered, with the impact of the teachers union's support for different aspects of the initiative, including greater teacher decision making and common planning, neutralized during the critical formative period of the academies, pending agreement on how to calculate common planning and similar responsibilities in a teacher's workload and resolution of other issues as part of a new contract. It has proven difficult also to abandon entrenched organizational structures—for example, to let go of schoolwide departments based on subject areas in favor of academy-based disciplinary and interdisciplinary teams—thus limiting academy-based decision making.

South High also has had to make hard choices, some made more difficult by an unexpectedly harsh reduction in budgetary resources over a period of several years. As part of the initiative, for example, South High aimed to increase the number of students progressing from college- to honors-level classes, and from honors-level to an expanded menu of advanced placement classes, using new strategically located forms of academic support. Leaders hoped that underperforming ninth-grade students would become strong achievers at the college level by participating in newly formed literacy and numeracy classes, and that students receiving support through the newly adopted "AVID" (Advancement Via Individual Determination) program would become solid honors and advanced placement students.[9] Staffing these programs in each academy, however, has proven problematic, as other responsibilities compete for teachers' time. The fallback plan has been to staff them on a limited basis, and resort to single classes that enroll students from all three academies; but this practice dilutes coherence in academy structures, cultures, and practice (see discussion of Jesse Weeks's teaching in Chapter 9).

Finally, there is the question of how to support equitable and effective teaching throughout South High, how to ensure, for example, that personalized attention to literacy development is integrated with content instruction. Literacy has been in the forefront of discussion since the school transformation initiative began, and is in the foreground of the school's required improvement plan. The Hiatt Center, through its professional development programs and graduate teaching interns, has provided assistance; and many of the center's teaching interns assigned at South, all taught to support literacy development in the process of instruction, have been hired. The academies have incorporated more writing activity across the curriculum as well as a scoring rubric to ensure clarity and consistency in writing across the 9th and 10th grades. Teachers are required to demonstrate their attention to literacy development in their planning. Promising steps all, but the process of infiltrating and transforming everyday practice in the name of literacy and equity requires concerted, sustained effort.[10] The process has been encumbered at South by lack of time for common planning and learning, and has competed with concern for fulfilling state and district curriculum mandates, a competition that forces a false choice between focusing on literacy or content standards as if they are mutually exclusive. During the 2008–09 school year, work began anew at South to make literacy development a central theme in professional learning and instruction with help from its university partner; every teacher will participate in professional learning in small teams with colleagues.

The Creation of Claremont Academy

While the ITA was forming at South, there was parallel work at the A.L.L. School. Already small in student population, the school designated its high school cluster, comprising about 240 students, the Co-NECT Academy. The Co-NECT academy introduced new literacy and portfolio assessment practices, as well as an "advisory" curriculum focused on assessing individual student academic progress, goals-setting, and skill development.

Unfortunately, however, the trajectory of development of the Co-NECT Academy flattened within a few years, until the Academy itself was left behind as part of yet another transition in the A.L.L. school's truncated history. As the systemwide high school reform initiative waned, the academy found itself caught in a web of countervailing forces. Out of concern for teacher workload, contractual negotiations suspended its advisory program for students, one of its key personalization practices. Hope for greater autonomy in decision making, in areas such as curriculum, scheduling, budgeting, professional development, and staff hiring was not fulfilled. As testing arrived in the wake of NCLB, the results were disappointing, particularly at the elementary and middle school levels. In 2005, after successive years of failure, the state affixed an underperformance label on the school and sent a fact-finding review team for an intensive 3-day visit. The team noted the lack of "an overarching, cohesive vision for this unique K–12 school" (Massachusetts Department of Elementary and Secondary Education, 2005,

p. 1). This was a critical blow. The Co-NECT Academy tried to argue its separateness from the rest of the school to no avail. The entire K–12 school rededicated attention to state standards and student readiness for state tests. Common planning time for the academy's teachers was a casualty, as the schedule and staff assignments were reshuffled to address different needs based on test performance. Finally, after long deliberation, the district and school committee decided to split up the school, creating Claremont Academy (Grades 7–12) and a separate K–6 academy.

Many educators have had their passions ignited by a reform initiative only to see them extinguished by forces out of their control. In its short burst of life, after only 6 years in its new building, the A.L.L. School had witnessed at least two of these cycles, had lived on the leading edge of educational reform only to see it crumble. Needless to say, some of the teachers who had "been there, done that" were numb with disillusion and low morale. But Claremont's Grade 7–12 configuration, constructed to parallel UPCS, set up a new opportunity to build continuity in culture and practice. Claremont began reorienting itself, once again, in the fall of 2006 with the Hiatt Center as a partner and with the principal of UPCS agreeing to serve simultaneously as its school leader. The challenging process of starting a new period of change has begun. During the 2008–09 school year the school instituted new academic support programs in literacy and numeracy and common planning time for teachers. A vanguard of three Claremont students enrolled in a course at the Clark University in the fall. About 50 students began either their second or third year of participation in the university mentor program, which serves students at UPCS as well. Several graduate teaching interns from the university helped in their classrooms. A university faculty member collaborated with two teachers to create a new transition-to-college course for 12th graders.

The Future Awaits for Main South High Schools

Clearly each of the schools of Main South carries a different weight of history in the process of reform. Perhaps South High labors under the heaviest burden. It is in a state of awkward though hopeful historical and cultural transition: beneath the demands of daily practice, there is a silent tug-of-war between limited resources and new planned opportunities for students, between residual beliefs, structures, and practices of the comprehensive high school and a new more egalitarian and transformative model, between past and future. Claremont Academy, with a handful of teachers who remember its short but concentrated history of false starts and fractured visions, must heal as it can, shake off any lingering doubts about its potential and the potential of its students, and persevere in remaking its culture of learning and achievement. UPCS has the advantage of following the historical and cultural course set at the moment of its conception.

If recent history suggests adversity and challenge, it also gives reason to believe in the value of transforming structure, culture, and practice. There is evidence in the data to suggest that efforts to enact principles of equity, personalization, literacy development, postsecondary readiness, teacher collaboration, community partnership, and elevated achievement for all students have had a beneficial effect. Data summarized in this chapter's Appendix reveal both positive trends and the continuing challenges that have to be met in order to write a new chapter of success. At UPCS, where these principles are most deeply ingrained in the culture, the record of student progress and achievement sets a resounding example. At Claremont Academy and South High the record suggests small but encouraging inroads during the past 5 years, the period during which the effort to apply these principles has been strongest.

But the story of challenge, change, and possibility in these schools and the many schools like them—how reform intersects with their different institutional histories and cultures—is written in actual practice more than in quantitative data. To understand better how the principles as well as purposes of reform get enacted in different contexts such as those represented by the Main South schools or, put differently, how diverse students with different needs are supported in learning, we need to look at the process more closely. We need to see it in all of its complexity and revealing detail, in the daily actions of teachers and students, and the worlds of learning created by them. The next chapter introduces the teachers at each of these schools whose classrooms we will briefly enter and some of the concepts and practices that inform their teaching.

APPENDIX: SUMMARY OF RECENT
DATA TRENDS AT CLAREMONT, SOUTH HIGH, AND UPCS

Below I summarize recent data on various indicators of school effectiveness collected by the Massachusetts Department of Elementary and Secondary Education, the Massachusetts Department of Higher Education, the Worcester Public Schools, and the Worcester Regional Research Bureau, Inc.[11] The recent collaborative effort of the Massachusetts Department of Elementary and Secondary Education and Massachusetts Department of Higher Education (2008) to understand the readiness of public high school graduates to complete entry-level course work at the state's 2- and 4-year colleges, reflected in the state's first school-to-college report, as noted in Chapter 1, signals the new emphasis on strengthening and supporting all students on the educational pathway to a postsecondary degree. I include here data that reveal the progress of Claremont, South High, and UPCS in fulfilling their respective role on that pathway.

Attendance

Data collection for Claremont Academy as a distinct school began in 2006–07. The attendance rate was 92.4% in that year, above the district high school average of 91.1%. South High, habitually below 90%, has reached that figure for 3 consecutive years (2004–2007). But its mobility rate—the combined percentage of students leaving and entering—has been at 50% or higher during that time, making progress in learning a moving target. UPCS, perennially atop the district, averages a 95% attendance rate and has a low mobility rate below 10%, which means that on average only 3-4 students leave or enter per year.

Statewide Test (MCAS) Scores

There are four categories of performance on the Massachusetts statewide tests: advanced, proficient, needs improvement, and warning/failure. In 2006–07 Claremont scores on the 10th grade English test were well above the district norm, and just below in mathematics. The majority of students scored in the advanced or proficient categories in English (71%) while 10% failed; 46% scored at the highest levels in mathematics while 22% failed. Performance was fairly even across subgroups, with low-income students as a whole performing slightly higher than Latino students. From 2004 to 2007 the percentage of South High students performing at the advanced or proficient levels in English increased steadily, reaching a majority by the end of that period, while the percentage of students failing declined. The trend is similar in mathematics, although the percentages are lower, with 44% of the students reaching the advanced or proficient levels in 2007. White and non-low-income students, however, outperform low-income, African American, and Latino students by a substantial margin. UPCS has the highest cumulative performance of any school serving a majority low-income population in the state, with 85% of students scoring at the advanced or proficient levels in English, and 81% in mathematics from 2002-2007. Students perform equally well regardless of ethnic subgroup. In 2007 UPCS was one of only three schools in the state in which every student passed a new biology test.

Advanced Placement Class Enrollment

UPCS has traditionally encouraged all of its students to enroll in challenging courses. In 2007, 31% of the high school students enrolled in an advanced placement class. In addition, about half the students in the graduating class successfully completed an introductory course at Clark University. South enrolled 17% of its students in an advanced placement class. While performance on the advanced placement tests is relatively low for students from both schools, the enrollment percentages are the highest in the district. At South in particular the enrollment percentage is indicative of recent effort to make rigorous courses accessible and reachable for more students. The challenge is to increase their preparedness for the classes as well as the support they receive while taking them. In 2006–07 only 7% of Claremont students enrolled in an advanced placement class; but that number increased to 18% (44 students of 240 enrolled in Grades 9–12) in 2007-08.

On-Time Graduation Rate

This refers to the percentage of students who begin in ninth grade and graduate within 4 years. The state has only recently collected this data. In 2007, the two smallest schools in the district, UPCS and Claremont, had the highest percentages, at 89.7% and 87.2%, respectively. South (68.1%) was second among the four former comprehensive high schools in the district, but overall its low rate points to persistent issues with mobility as well as retention, particularly with regard to Latino students.

Postgraduation Plans and College Readiness

The state collects data on students' postgraduation intentions. From 2003 to 2007, UPCS had the highest percentage of students in the district planning to attend a 2- or 4-year college (100% for 4 out of 5 years). South's record is uneven, but overall it has progressed from 79% to 95% during that time. The Claremont record is also uneven, but reached 92 and 96% during the 5-year period, which include its prior life as the Co-NECT Academy. While these figures do not reflect actual matriculation rates, they point to a trend in aspiration that suggests that the original purposes of the academies at Claremont and South to elevate the educational trajectories of Main South students are manifesting in some way in their cultures. According to the state's first school-to-college report, 51% of South High students and 39% of UPCS students (from the class of 2005) enrolling in public postsecondary institutions needed to take a developmental or remedial course. To put the UPCS record in perspective, the entire graduating class qualified for postsecondary learning at a 2- or 4-year college during that year. Based on feedback from a survey administered in 2007–08, we estimate that 10% of all UPCS alumni, whether attending state or nonstate colleges, have been required to take a remedial course.

CHAPTER 3

The Teachers, Shared Concepts, and Collaborative Learning

IN CHAPTERS 4 through 9 we will enter the classrooms of seven teachers, two each from Claremont and South High and three from UPCS. My observations are based mainly on one or two class sessions, but are given depth by my background knowledge of the teachers—all of whom I have known for their entire careers—and the evolution of their practice and their schools. In many cases my observations benefited from the eyes and ears of other observers who attended the classes with me, usually some combination of teachers, graduate teaching interns, and colleagues from Clark University. These co-observers were looking in particular at aspects of the learning process that were of concern to the host classroom teacher, as part of a collaborative learning practice we call "Rounds," which I will describe below.

My observations are also reflective, as I try to shed light on some of the inner and outer dynamics of teaching practice, by which I mean the complex of factors that inform and shape a teacher's work with subject matter and students and, therefore, her or his efforts to ensure opportunity and equity in learning. I aim to bring into view various dimensions of teaching—its daily challenge, contours, textures, and contextures—and to examine how belief, thought, action, setting, and policy interact and influence one another. The schools—historically and culturally different, yet all serving students with a similar demographic profile, most living in the same or adjoining neighborhoods of Main South—afford a unique set of vantage points for understanding this interplay.

THE TEACHERS

The teachers have much in common. All of them have worked in some collaborative fashion with faculty at the Hiatt Center. Five of the seven have graduate degrees in teaching or education from Clark University; one, at the time of my visit to his class, was in the Master of Arts in Teaching program. As a result of this background their practice is framed by similar beliefs and working assumptions. They believe that each student is a capable thinker, with distinct strengths, personal qualities, and backgrounds that can be leveraged in learning; that, to the extent they develop a trusting relationship, they can help a student bring himself or herself more fully to learning. They believe that learning is a social and value-laden process as well as an individual intellectual one; they draw on students' diverse backgrounds and experiences to reinforce the importance of an integrated community as part of learning. They believe that learning should be meaningful, that the personal and academic should connect and lead to student understandings that open an ever-widening view of themselves and the world. They strive to enlarge students' capacities for learning, to provide them in particular with the academic tools to understand and develop sophisticated ideas: to become careful readers, writers, and speakers who can express their thinking in honest and academically valid ways. They believe that all of their students can and should qualify for some form of postsecondary education. A developmental perspective of learning textures these beliefs: The teachers understand where students are in their development as thinkers and academic learners and where they need to go, and are constantly at work on the steps that will get them there.

Nevertheless, the teachers and their teaching are affected, in subtle as well as obvious ways, by differences in their individual school histories and cultures, by their tenure at the schools, and by their own level of experience. They also represent four different subject areas and different grade levels, part of my effort to capture a broad range of teaching experience across the schools and add to the layers of questions that need to be confronted in addressing reform in a school setting. Kate Shepard, a 9-year veteran, teaches 7th- and 8th-grade mathematics at UPCS. Adelina Zaimi, a 2nd-year teacher at Claremont, teaches 9th-grade algebra. Jody Bird, a veteran of 8 years, teaches 9th-grade biology at UPCS. Chris Rea is teaching 11th-grade physics as a graduate teaching intern at South High. Chad Malone, also a 2nd-year teacher at Claremont, teaches English language arts at several grade levels; he was a graduate teaching intern at UPCS. Ricci Hall, who began his teaching career at UPCS in the school's inaugural year 11 years ago, teaches 11th- and 12th-grade history. Jesse Weeks is in his 5th year as a 9th-grade history teacher at South High. Except for Adelina, who is an adult immigrant from Albania, all these teachers are native English speakers. The teachers otherwise have White middle-class backgrounds, a profile typical among adults at their schools.

SHARED CONCEPTS

There are several concepts that recur in my discussion of teaching practice. These represent understandings about curriculum and learning that the teachers and I share, and that we use as shorthand in our partnership discourse. I introduce several of them here, but otherwise explain them, as necessary, as they surface in the discussions of teaching.

Content standards are a familiar concept to most educators, and usually refer to the particular subject matter knowledge that students must learn, per local requirements. The term *standard* may refer in addition to expected social and civic behaviors, but when I use the term, I am referring to content. Although I sometimes use the term in a generic sense, in most cases I am referring to those standards specified in the Massachusetts "curriculum frameworks"—the summary of curriculum principles and concepts that the state has developed for each subject area and grade level—since they form the basis of the accountability system for the teachers. In several instances I use content standards to refer to the specific interpretation of the state curriculum frameworks at the local district level. This should be clear from context.

The *disciplinary way of knowing* refers to the process of learning that is followed in each discipline and forms the epistemology or dynamic origin of subject matter knowledge. As one dimension of its way of knowing, for example, science combines an attitude of skepticism with a tightly orchestrated experimental methodology. Scientists presume that something might not be true even as they engage in finding out whether it is; they try to determine what the physical evidence says, at the same time that they endeavor to show that it cannot be otherwise. And this process is governed by different protocols and forms of validation that have been developed by real people over time. Students who learn the disciplinary way of knowing of science, in effect learning to think and act like scientists, will understand and be able to practice this process to some degree. They will be able to show whether a conclusion based on physical evidence is likely to be valid or not. They will have in some sense "disciplined" their minds—developed *disciplinary habits of mind and learning*. The ways of knowing of the historian, the mathematician, the literary reader, the artist, and the musician are likewise distinct. This dynamic in the formation of knowledge—the actual intellectual give-and-take in its development—is often hidden from students in school curriculum. Yet it can be represented. It can enliven study by immersing students in real problems in engaging ways, so as to build a bridge between their curiosity, their questions, and their experience and disciplined inquiry, and develop particular habits of mind and academic competence together with understanding. By teaching fundamental aspects of the disciplinary ways of knowing, teachers do not simply introduce students to the world of knowledge, they induct them slowly into the worlds of knowledge making and knowledge use, putting them in a much more empowering position intellectually, academically, and socially. Knowledge is not something handed to them, but is the result of human effort conducted in a social context with real consequences for people and the natural environment, in which they, too, have a stake and take part.

Literacy development has become an increasingly prominent theme in discussions of high school learning and curriculum. There is substantial work in research and pedagogy addressing the distinct literacy needs of adolescents.[1] Those students who enter high school reading and writing below grade level may disconnect from school rather than disclose their shortcomings. What is certain is that they will have difficulty with academic texts and discourse, and without a teacher who can help bridge their self-perceptions and a positive identity as academic learners, they are in danger of falling irretrievably behind. Even students who read and write with some fluency may have difficulty with academic texts and academic discourse. Like underprepared students, they need support for developing *academic literacy*, the literacy embedded in each academic subject, as distinct from the literacy of home, social group, or the Internet, which students otherwise master.

Teachers attuned to the importance of integrating academic literacy development with content learning and the disciplinary way of knowing provide support for the development of all students as readers, writers, and speakers as a matter of course. They are aware, as well, that even students who appear proficient can progress in their academic literacy development, that these students, too, are underserved if not challenged to master the academic discourse that characterizes advanced formal learning. Academic literacy represents the idea that students need tools of literacy as well as other habits of thinking and doing that build confidence, care, and competence in formal learning.

At different times I refer to *authentic or meaningful learning*. By this I mean, in general, opportunities for students to freely and honestly engage their minds and sensibilities with subject matter that is real to them, and for good purpose. In authentic learning students strive to answer questions, solve problems, and construct understandings that are foundational in the field of study. Their own ideas and questions are respected, encouraged, and part of the process; they can bring themselves fully to the learning. They learn disciplinary ways of knowing, and become increasingly better thinkers, readers, writers, speakers, questioners, and problem solvers.

As significant as these developments are, however, they hold deeper lessons: learning that is authentic has implications beyond the intellectual and academic. Teacher and students care about each other and what they are learning; students gain a sense of community and its value. More broadly, students learn to distinguish what is important from what is not, likely from unlikely, genuine from disingenuous, and true from false, and value doing so. They learn to recognize and surmount arbitrary or artificial limits, whether those are imposed from without or from within. As a result, students become more familiar with the breadth and depth of their own capacities and capabilities and learn to measure their own possibilities in ever larger terms. In the totality of this process, cumulatively over time, they can become more authentic themselves and deepen their understanding of what it means to be a free yet connected and responsible person living in community. Authentic learning is based on respect for students as they are and for the process of becoming more fully and consequentially human. It brings schooling in line with the deeper purposes of education, making it a vital expression of what it means to live, in particular what it means to live in a democratic and globally responsible society.

COLLABORATIVE LEARNING PRACTICES

Teachers need *collaborative learning practices*. Most professions have recognized practices for generating and sharing knowledge. The field of education draws heavily on the social sciences as well as experimental design for its research paradigm. Consequently, the development of teaching practice is often characterized in terms of applying the findings of basic research. But the path of application is not always well-defined and does not easily adapt to the different cultural terrain of different schools. Furthermore, this path neglects the knowledge that resides in practice and the practitioner: tacit or clinical forms of knowledge cultivated in fields such as medicine or engineering, often in confrontation with unique problems or situations, a familiar occurrence for teachers.[2] While some try to harvest this knowledge in collegial forms of professional sharing and learning, it is done all too rarely in comparison to traditional research, and more rarely still in collaborative fashion within a university. The profession needs collaborative modes of learning about and developing practice that lie close to the ground—learning that brings together research, practice, theory, context, and policy and builds the professional community of practice within and across schools. Practice can be fertile ground for understanding learning and teaching, for cultivating knowledge that is useful in the particular classroom and school context in which it emerges, and conceivably beyond. The added benefit of practice-based knowledge is that it is immediately accessible to and owned by teachers, enhancing its potential impact.

The partnership world defined by a school and university creates a unique potential to nurture both useful understandings about practice and collaborative ways for developing and sharing them. In the Hiatt Center partnership there are a number of collaborative learning practices that bring together the world of the university and the classroom. These practices explore the blurred edges of theory, teaching practice, and context, where they are in constant interplay, informing and merging into each other. They foster mutual understanding and relationship, on the one hand, and, on the other, a culture of knowledge exchange and knowledge development. I explain several of these practices in the chapters on teaching, as they bear on the question of how good teaching develops and gets sustained, so I introduce them only briefly here.

Our most prominent collaborative learning practice is *Rounds* (Del Prete, 1997). A familiar practice in hospital-based medical training, our version of Rounds gathers a small group of colleagues for focused classroom-based observation and reflection. Typically, teachers from a partner school and the university join together with graduate students to comprise the collegial group. By design, this composition builds several different, complementary, and mutually informing perspectives into the process of inquiry and reflective observation fostered by the Round. When Rounds become habitual, this process becomes more deeply ingrained in the collaborative work of a school and/or a partnership, and, as in our case, the various perspectives begin to form a shared and expandable base of understanding with respect to good teaching and its development.

A Round is hosted by a teacher or student in the Master of Arts in Teaching program (referred to as an "MAT" or "graduate teaching intern"). The host teacher prepares a short Round sheet for the Round group that summarizes the background (students' academic development, the curriculum) and learning focus (the goals, learning process, and general rationale) of the class. To frame the inquiry process of the Round, the teacher also identifies a set of questions (usually 3–5) critical to understanding the learning process in the class. These questions often ask observers to look and listen for specific signs of student learning in keeping with the focus and goals of the lesson. For example, in a class in which students are examining a primary source in history, the Round host teacher might ask: Are all students using textual clues to determine the author's point of view? Are they discussing what these clues reveal about the author's bias and intent? Are students comparing their written ideas about how contemporary events (specified by the teacher) may have shaped or been shaped by the primary source? Do they compare the source to other sources that they have been asked to examine and draw specific conclusions or ask questions based on the comparison? Answers to questions such as these can shed light on how, to what extent, and with what purpose students are engaged in learning and developing understanding. Often, in addition, the host teacher asks for feedback on whether a particular aspect of his or her teaching practice has had the desired impact. Thus the Round sheet is a means of reviewing and reflecting on goals and planning, forming a habit of inquiry focused on observable or readily obtainable evidence of student learning, and sharing and developing practice with others.

The Round sheet becomes the basis for a pre-Round discussion, usually of 15 or 20 minutes duration, in which all participants work to understand the planning and thought process of the teacher, and identify the observation data that will be useful for addressing the teacher's Round questions as well as how to obtain this data (e.g., by observing a single student or asking students questions). Occasionally the pre-Round discussion leads to some changes in the original plan, as ideas emerge in the process of explaining and clarifying the lesson. The goal is to make the teacher's thought process and practice as clear and transparent as possible. A post-Round discussion occurs after the Round observation. The host teacher usually begins the discussion, sharing observations to which the Round participants add, and asking for observations related to the Round questions. Unanticipated yet valuable topics invariably enter the conversation.

Rounds serve a variety of purposes in our partnership, but primarily they are a means for sharing, inquiring into, and advancing practice and, not least, for developing the habit of doing so. They are a key ingredient in the development of the professional learning cultures within partner schools and the partnership as a whole and in the development of the MATs as teachers. They often combine with other learning practices to make professional learning a multifaceted and continuous process with real classroom impact. That said, Rounds is not a simple practice to introduce, as practicing teachers as well as teaching interns understandably feel vulnerable, particularly with unfamiliar colleagues. Also, Rounds tend to be more representative of a teacher's actual practice and most beneficial—generating honest, open, respectful, and constructive conversation—if they are done frequently as a regular professional practice, as they are at UPCS. A teacher and her students might otherwise feel on display and strain to do something extraordinary.

Graduate teaching interns such as Chris Rea also do Rounds at regular intervals and attend each other's Rounds. This process is heightened by the team-based model followed in their Master of Arts in Teaching program. During his graduate teaching internship, for example, Chris was joined at South High by nine other students in the university Master of Arts in Teaching program. They began their teaching assignments at South High at the very beginning of the school year and continued through the end of the university academic year, in early May. They participated together in a variety of school-based activities in the program as they learned the process, represented by Rounds, of observing, reflecting, questioning, and understanding teaching and learning, and of developing their teaching practice individually and collaboratively as members of a professional community.

Most of the classroom observations that I discuss in this book occurred in the context of a Round. For all of the teachers involved, a Round is a familiar and routine experience; Jody, Kate, and Ricci have hosted dozens. Many of the Rounds would have occurred whether or not I attended. I respected and wanted to capture this normalcy and authenticity as much as possible. In most cases I mentioned my interest in writing about the Round just before it occurred, but with no elaboration so as to minimize any influence on the teacher's prior planning; in the cases of Chris and Chad I mentioned it afterward. The teachers readily agreed; I was a familiar participant in Rounds they had hosted or attended in the past. I took notes like everyone else, but more detailed in my case. These notes, together with notes from pre-Round and post-Round discussions, formed the primary basis of my description of their teaching. I wove these together with what I knew from observing and discussing their teaching with them on other occasions, in most cases over a period of years.

Most of the teachers also are involved in other collaborative learning practices of the Hiatt Center *Curriculum Teams*, organized by discipline (history, humanities, mathematics, and the physical and natural sciences), bring together university and school teachers, including arts and sciences faculty from the university, for common investigation of core content concepts, the disciplinary way of knowing, and exemplary curriculum and practice. I describe the teams in more detail in the discussion of Adelina's teaching (Chapter 5). At the annual *Best Practice Workshop,* teachers share and discuss a particular aspect of their practice with each other. Many teachers also serve as *Mentor Teachers*, mentoring a graduate student like Chris in collaboration with a Hiatt faculty member. Finally, to varying degrees and in various ways, they also take on coinstructional roles in the Master of Arts in Teaching program, again working collaboratively with a faculty member from the Hiatt Center.

The development, articulation, and dissemination of usable knowledge about teaching practice is a critical need, particularly in light of standards, accountability systems, teacher development, and the goals and hopes for reform.[3] Collaborative learning practices such as the ones in our partnership encourage this development. They provide conduits for informal and formal exchanges that enrich dialogue and understanding in the specific and familiar contexts in which teachers work, and they have the potential to produce ideas for more widespread consumption. At UPCS they help build the schoolwide culture of learning for students as well as teachers.

The reflective observations on teaching in the chapters that follow add to our partnership's collaborative learning repertoire and are a preliminary step in pushing this idea forward. I have tried to use my vantage point and privileged understanding of the teachers and their work to illuminate areas of teaching that otherwise might be hidden from view. The teachers involved have read and given feedback on my write-ups, both verbally and in writing. The most elaborate feedback came from Chris Rea. He interspersed his written comments with my own; I have included several of them in the text, to represent his insight (Chapter 7). To a significant extent, then, the teachers and I learned together.

CHAPTER 4

Everyone Has a Seat at the Table: Kate Shepard's Mathematics Learning Community

PICK A RANDOM moment during this class, and the chances are high that you will see Kate Shepard kneeling close to a cluster of three desks, eye to eye with her students, asking whether something makes sense, or listening to a student's explanation of how to make the "jump" from 5 to 10 in the banquet table problem that they have been presented today, or encouraging students to think or talk or write. The short moments in between are punctuated with reminders to the whole class that "this is silent thinking time," exhortations to "talk, talk, talk," or "write, write, write," or fervent affirmations in the form of "good thinking" or "good job." Occasionally she urges a single student or one of the groups of three to try to find yet another way to solve the banquet table problem, instigating a fresh pondering of all the information at hand. At a few junctures, Kate is in front of the class coaxing students to give her all their different ways of thinking about and figuring out the problem, as she clarifies and writes them down for all to consider. When student-generated "rules" fill the whiteboard, turning it into a mathematical cornucopia, she asks students to decide which way is the simplest. Students pause to examine their collective effort, searching for the single most congenial rule to cover all the different cases the problem entails.

The students themselves are fully complicit. They follow the self-described "crazy woman" with a concentrated and studied air, offering their ideas more or less readily, some more soft-spoken, others more self-assured. By the arrival of this April day in their math class, they are accustomed to the themes of writing and talking, thinking and figuring out. They are tall, short, and in between, awkward, knowing, innocent, and many-hued. As seventh graders at University Park Campus School they have learned that their ideas will be taken seriously, that math involves looking at relationships among things that can be put into the form of words as well as numbers, or symbols and graphic illustrations. And further, they have come to believe there is more than one way to figure these things out, and that even ways that do not work have some value in finding ways that do. Among the 20 students, 11 girls and 9 boys, there may be momentary looks of perplexity, but no one appears truly worried or lost. The students clearly have confidence in their teacher and in themselves.

What mountaineering guides are to wary climbers, Kate is to these students. She is at home in her rugged and—for many of her charges—forbidding terrain, and a tireless, unfailingly reliable, and cheerful companion in exploring it; she adapts to what her group needs, adjusting her guidance to the challenges of the journey. She and her seventh-grade charges have traveled a long way together, have developed group routines, expanded expectations, and acquired the habits of mathematical thinking necessary to meet them, have learned to work collaboratively, and have cultivated a thorough understanding of number sense as a prelude to today's excursion into algebra via the banquet table problem.

THE BANQUET TABLE PROBLEM

Kate uses the banquet table problem as a gateway to the study of patterns and functions and as one in a steady diet of activities through which she very deliberately aims to develop her students' identities and capabilities as mathematical thinkers. In the Round sheet that she has prepared for this class, one among many that she routinely develops to share her practice with university students preparing to teach mathematics, she explains, "This problem has become a vital part of my curriculum. I find that it lays the foundation for many algebraic concepts and skills."

The problem—her favorite, as she affectionately introduces it—has a certain seductive charm. In a magical kingdom whose residents happily immerse themselves in mathematical problem solving "all the time, all day" and frequently celebrate their accomplishments in banquets hosted by their beaming king and queen, the most difficult job might be that held by the "table inputter"—the numerically minded manager who must have the requisite number of tables and seats ready for each festive gathering. As the banquet follows traditional regal decorum, the tables must be set end to end, creating a single-table effect in the long banquet hall. The crowd presses to enter on the latest occasion, and the table manager must determine quickly the number of seats available as servants march tables into the hall. The students are called upon to help. Can they figure out how many of the kingdom's subjects can be seated if there is a certain number of tables?

Kate swiftly draws a square on the whiteboard to represent a single table, representing four seats, and then adds two more, using perpendicular lines to indicate each seat (see Figure 4.1). As students tell her the number of people who can be seated at the growing line of tables she records the data on a T-chart.

She then asks students to figure out for themselves the number of people who can sit at 4 or 5 tables and then "jump" to 10 tables. "No talking— silent thinking time right now—then [I will] tell you, OK, it's time to talk." She passes out bags of multicolored squares for students who want to use them to represent tables; students have more than one way to look at the problem.

One student works first from the T-chart to a sketch of tables, and proceeds to a written explanation of how he arrived at the number of people that 10 tables will accommodate: "for every single table, you add two more people, like 4,6,8,10,12, jump 22." Next to him a student lines up tables with the squares and counts the places. Kate says to the class, "After you get to 10, give me some words—write, write, write." Some time later she observes, "I see some different methods . . . OK, you can talk."

MATHEMATICAL THINKING AND WRITING

Writing integrates seamlessly into students' learning in Kate's class. Together with talking and graphic illustration, it is used as a tool to express and clarify thinking, and to explain, develop, and share ideas. Students' seeming facility, however, is deceiving; what began as an unnatural act has become a habit of learning only through Kate's patient insistence; single words in math journal entries have been fertilized and stretched into sentences and illustrated explanations through carefully nurtured effort.

Most students do not enter Kate's class with a view of math and writing as compatible activities. They must learn that math is more than numbers, that mathematical thinking and writing go hand in hand, and that numbers in various combinations and relationships become all the more intelligible and familiar when you have written about them and developed them to some extent yourself. And if you have tried to explain them to someone puzzling over them as you have, or teetering on the cusp of clarity, then there is a potential double dose of learning. One of Kate's signature requirements is to ask students to write a letter to someone who does not quite understand one or another aspect of the mathematics under study. These "Dear Confused" letters illuminate the reasoning behind solutions to problems such as the banquet table in various personal ways. If, upon reading them, Kate herself is confused by an explanation, then she adds a note or question, and a short written exchange between teacher and student follows until some mutually satisfying clarity forms.

Figure 4.1. Kate's Banquet Table and T-Chart

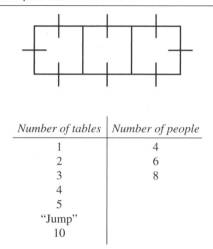

Number of tables	Number of people
1	4
2	6
3	8
4	
5	
"Jump"	
10	

As they get accustomed to explaining and thinking with the tip of their pencils, writing for Kate's students becomes a normal part of learning. This cognitive process is not confined to mathematics, as students engage in variations of Kate's "writing-to-learn" activities in other classes. Writing "across the curriculum" is standard fare at UPCS. On any given day it is likely that students will be writing down their thinking in science, or in response to a provocative prompt in history, or for some other explanatory or exploratory purpose. Just a week after Kate's class, during a Round hosted by one of the MAT students, seventh graders engage in a lively exchange of early drafts of persuasive essays, developed in a "writers' workshop" format. Hung in one corner, a banner announces, "We are Writers. Welcome to our Sanctuary." Writing is fast forming a community based on the development and exchange of new ideas.

Many of the writing assignments at UPCS are "low stakes," with little or no consequence for grades, yet with significance for learning and participation in the learning community. Teachers routinely give them as one way to make students' thinking visible, and review them for purposes of understanding the development of students' understanding rather than formal evaluation. Low stakes enhances the prospect for some expression of genuine thinking rather than something calculated to make a grade. Writing-to-learn activities thus have a dual character, both personal expressions and expressions of content understanding in formation. Customary and trusted at UPCS, they play an important long-term role in the formation of students' habits of mind, and their thoughtfulness and confidence as school learners.

They help draw each student personally into the academic world, affirming their place in it and building a vital connection.

That these seventh-grade students will have Kate as their eighth-grade teacher as well—a process called *looping*—has enormous impact on their learning; that they will meet with her for 75-minute classes, as compared to the 60-minute norm, only amplifies the benefits of having her for 2 years. Most entered UPCS as resistant or insecure math learners. Continuity in expectation, routines, and curriculum will help ensure that they progress steadily in the algebraic thinking that they apply in solving the banquet table problem, and build the foundation they need for more advanced mathematical study. The mutual familiarity that teacher and students develop over the course of 2 years will inform the myriad adjustments of support for each of them that Kate will make.

EVERYONE'S IDEAS COUNT

After a short period of desk talk during which students tell each other the methods they have tried to determine the number of places available at 10 tables, Kate draws the attention of the class to the front of the room. "Let's hear lots of methods," she urges. One student explains how she "counted around the edges" of the table. Kate pauses to let this explanation hang for a moment in the fertile intellectual air of the class; she then asks students for a word to describe what this one student has done and hears "perimeter" in reply. It is an indication of a student appropriating knowledge of arithmetic and geometry in solving the problem, a prealgebraic method, but one that makes sense, particularly at this point in the students' learning. Another says that she "noticed there was a pattern" while working with four tables, and "figured out ten [places]." One noticed on the T-chart that the numbers "increase by two in the right column and by one in the left." Kate asks for a full explanation of these and other different methods and carefully illustrates them on the whiteboard.

At this stage in the lesson, students are becoming familiar with the content, with the lay of the land. There is ample room to explore, to follow one way that seems accessible and workable, and also to retrace that route for others to consider. Many students have something to offer and each one's approach is respected and validated, uncovering some of the many pathways one can take in solving this problem. There is time to learn about the students' different pathways, thereby making new connections to the problem and expanding the possibilities for describing the relationships involved with numbers. In taking this approach, Kate both creates room for everyone's participation and makes the notion of *function* that will eventually emerge more accessible and understandable. Everyone's ideas count, everyone can feel some relationship to the slow building of mutual understanding. Everyone belongs; there is a place for everyone at this table. As a result, this does not feel like an academic exercise so much as an active and respectful learning community. These goals are explicit and central in Kate's Round sheet:

> My main goal is to build confidence [by] giving students a task they can all engage and succeed in. Second to that, students will be able to:
>
> - Investigate patterns
> - Create algebraic rules to describe a functional relationship
> - Begin to connect problem situations, diagrams, tables, rules, and graphs
> - Write and interpret algebraic formulas like $y = 4x + 2$ or $y = (s\text{-}2)x + 2$ and show an understanding of the mathematical notation

They are also reflected in Kate's Round questions:

1. Is it true that all students are able to safely engage in this problem and learn some mathematics? Explain what you observe that applies to this question.
2. Record quotes or occurrences that demonstrate how students are learning from one another.
3. How is the whole-class discussion piece going? Are students listening to one another? Am I asking questions that require students to share their thinking? Are various methods explained fully? Do students seem to understand the discussion?
4. Record any needs you see. What needs to happen to ensure all students reach their highest potential?

Having seen evidence that students understand the problem and ways to solve it, Kate judges them ready for a new level of challenge in the task. She has designed the next stage of the class to encourage algebraic thinking and move students toward the formulation of an algebraic rule. Kate asks students to figure out how many people can be seated at 100 tables. Writing again serves as handmaiden to thinking, as Kate requires a letter to the kingdom's function coordinator that explains how to find the number of people at any given number of tables. "See if you can include a 'rule' in your letter. . . . If you can write three letters with three different [rules] that would be cool! You want to be hired!" There is another period of silent thinking time and student-to-student talk, with Kate circulating, crouching, listening, encouraging, and asking for explanation and elaboration. To one group she asks, "Can you tell me why you do that?" To another, apparently done with sharing ideas, she suggests finding an alternative way. In these interactions Kate is "assessing"—not in the sense of testing, of course, as it is commonly viewed, but in its root meaning of "sitting beside." *To assess* as Kate does during the class means traveling alongside students on their journeys of learning, and being attuned to what they are thinking and understanding, so as to determine what they might need and are ready to do next. Assessment in this sense is highly personalized, and Kate practices it in a pure form, as diligently as any doctor or any other professional who needs both an intimate knowledge of their field and of those they serve in order to do their work well.

Still, reflecting on what happened afterwards, Kate feels that in one instance she missed an opportunity for considering with the class the inadequacies of one student's approach. This student determined that 100 tables will seat 220 patrons. Kate asks whether this student can tell another student "why" she chose to do what she did in making the calculation, in hopes that the act of explaining will cause some revisiting and rethinking of the method the student used. Then Kate bends close and says, "Let me see if I understand. . . . It makes sense to me. . . . Does it make sense? Why not? Think about it, think about it." Kate chooses on this occasion to step away from the student and let her figure out with her partner what she has done. In retrospect she wishes that she had made this a matter for whole-group consideration. She does double back to the student's solution and reasoning much later in the class. The problem becomes an object lesson for how what seems to make sense is not always what works. To get 220, the student multiplied the number of seats at 10 tables (22) by 10. This solution was elegant mathematically, but neglected to take into account that each set of 10 tables, set end to end, loses 2 seats. Kate emphasizes what has been learned in the act of pursuing what turns out to be a false promise. On the one hand, it "reflects good thinking, gets us to look at more math . . . but you have to check and see if it works."

In her illuminating essay, "The Virtues of Not Knowing," Eleanor Duckworth (1996) describes Alec, a boy "who would be any teacher's joy" (p. 67). Accustomed to being right in his judgments and to the acquiescence of his classmates, Alec one day finds himself standing alone. He and his fellow 10-year-old students are puzzling over the question of whether a pendulum slows down at either end of its swing, or simply reverses course while keeping its speed constant. Alec takes the latter position. One by one, however, others adopt the view that the pendulum does slow down, swayed more by their observations than Alec's deductive approach. They move from blind faith to uncertainty, and eventually to new conviction. This episode takes on the character of a parable, as Duckworth summarizes it,

> The class played out in public view virtues concerned with courage, caution, confidence, and risk. . . .The courage to submit an idea of one's own to someone else's scrutiny is a virtue in itself—unrelated to the rightness of the idea. Alec's idea was wrong, but it was his customary willingness to propose it and defend it that paved the way for a more accurate idea. The other children were right, but they would never have arrived at that right idea if they had not taken the risk—both within themselves and in public—to question Alec's idea.
>
> . . . The virtues involved in not knowing are the ones that really count in the long run . . . accepting surprise, puzzlement, excitement, patience, caution, honest attempts, and wrong outcomes as legitimate and important elements of learning, easily leads to their further development. (pp. 68–69)

Kate was disappointed in the timing of her response to the 220-seat solution. She did not address it immediately, but only when it occurred to her that she might illustrate for the class the value of the virtues of not knowing even after the most pregnant moment had passed. Her dissatisfaction is a testament to her determination to make thinking a central feature of the learning culture, to make exploration of content terrain fruitful for everyone.

Kate's class progresses through two more stages of learning. First, students offer various rules for determining the number of seats available at any given number of tables. An eager student tells how she figured out the number of seats at 100 tables. Kate asks, "Why does it make sense to do 100 times 2 plus 2?" The student relies on a visual representation of the tables to illustrate the process. Her classmates offer alternative methods, such as "$n + n + 1 + 1$," with n representing the number of seats along one side of the length of the banquet table. Several other methods are explained, illustrated, affirmed. Kate concludes, "Look at all these different rules. Are you telling me that all these rules work for the same problem? All of these [produce] the right answer?. . . If these are all right, do they all mean the same thing? What is the most simplified form of all?" After wrapping up this collective effort, with agreement on "$2n + 2$" as an economical rule, Kate complicates the problem one more time. "You think they only have square tables?" She passes out bags full of pentagons, triangles, and hexagons, and asks students to determine rules using each of these polygons. Students work on this challenging variation of the banquet table problem until Kate ends the class with, "Good job today. You did a lot of good thinking. [We'll] share some ideas tomorrow."

OPENING UP LEARNING FOR ALL

Kate's teaching reverses the reform paradox that narrows the scope of a student's learning in the name of fulfilling standards or preparing for high-stakes tests. Rather than press for quick and expedient solutions, Kate opens up the learning experience and, by doing so, expands the possibility for learning. Her practice is the antithesis of one-dimensional, one-size-fits-all teaching. What helps shape it? First of all, Kate is confident with her subject matter and how to expose its conceptual terrain to students. She also believes that learning involves understanding and that understanding can only come about when each student is supported along his or her personal path of knowing. When Kate shifts focus in the banquet table problem from 10 to 100 tables, increasing the level of challenge, as it were, by a factor of 10, she does so based on her students' understanding, not an arbitrary timetable; in the class, she moves from one phase of learning to the next at carefully cultivated moments of student readiness. Kate believes as well that learning is a social act and that students can learn from each other's different cognitive forays into a subject, thus benefiting when they are supported in learning from and with each other. Personalized and communalized forms of knowing are two parts of a whole; both are necessary conditions in Kate's class for the development of formal knowledge in mathematics. In her vision of a potent learning culture, personalized knowing, developing formal knowledge, a supportive learning community, and equity go hand in hand.

For teachers who are consumed by test results and feel pressured by the constraints of time to cover the curriculum with relentless speed, Kate's philosophy of learning and pedagogy may be as counterintuitive as the idea that a pendulum slows down at the end of its swing was to Alec in Duckworth's example. Many adopt a much more directive mode of teaching, for which problems like the banquet table become superfluous: Simply supply students with the most elegant solution in the first place, all will follow along dutifully, and all will be well; expediency assumes an air of philosophy. Kate's practice, in contrast, is multidimensional, joining together personal and collective effort in tasks that align with big ideas in the content (for example, functions) while accommodating diverse ways of thinking about and accomplishing them. Her students learn to think more flexibly, to examine a problem from its different sides. In the constant flow and explanation of ideas they learn the subject matter terrain, what makes sense as a way through it, and why. They develop tolerance and appreciation for both divergent and convergent thinking. As ninth graders they will take algebra with one of Kate's like-minded colleagues and their progress will continue. Most will pass the state test at a high level. More important, many, as juniors and seniors, will qualify to take courses in mathematics, science, and the social sciences at Clark University, all of which require sound mathematical thinking.

The Massachusetts standards in mathematics neither strongly support nor seriously constrain Kate's pedagogy. Judging by the principles, they are fully compatible with her understanding of mathematics learning. The very first guiding principle states:

> To achieve mathematical understanding, students should be actively engaged in doing meaningful mathematics, discussing mathematical ideas, and applying mathematics in interesting, thought-provoking situations. . . . Tasks should be designed to challenge students in multiple ways. Short- and long-term investigations that connect procedures and skills with conceptual understanding are integral components of an effective mathematics program. Activities should build upon curiosity and prior knowledge, and enable students to solve progressively deeper, broader, and more sophisticated problems. (Massachusetts Department of Elementary and Secondary Education, 2000, p. 7)

In the seventh- and eighth-grade curriculum guidelines for which Kate is responsible, there is a section on "exploratory concepts and skills" that reinforces this principle, with verbs such as *investigate, explore,* and *apply* introducing desirable activities in patterns, relations, algebra, geometry, measurement, data analysis, statistics, and probability. The actual learning standards use a more performance-based language, such as "demonstrate," "identify," and "define," language that evokes the test students will take.

Viewed as a philosophical system, the principles, learning standards, and exploratory concepts in the mathematics curriculum frameworks hold together and reflect the intention to represent mathematics as "an integrated field of study" (Massachusetts, 2000, p. 6). Still, it is not a simple matter to implement them coherently and in an integrated way. Focus tends to be more on the performances expected than on developing the conceptual understanding that leads to them. And if teachers themselves have learned in a context in which procedure and performance are emphasized over mathematical thinking, the prospects for the multidimensional teaching implied in the curriculum frameworks considered as a whole dim. Unfortunately, teachers in the United States are more likely to have learned math procedurally than conceptually, as reported in *The Teaching Gap* (1999), Stigler and Hiebert's comparative study of mathematics teaching in Japan, Germany, and the United States (see discussion in Chapter 5). This approach is far from what many mathematicians themselves would endorse, as I was able to confirm in a conversation with several colleagues in the Mathematics Department at Clark University. None had read *The Teaching Gap*, but one knows Kate as a coparticipant on the Mathematics Curriculum Team sponsored by the Hiatt Center. These mathematicians do not view math in terms of either procedure or performance. They emphasize the importance of mathematical thinking and knowing a few simple principles and geometric arguments deeply, understanding their influence on "everything else," and being able to apply them widely, rather than "memorize" them. One mathematician explains that difficult problems can be solved easily by algorithms; another asserts the importance of connecting the concrete to the abstract; a third tells how he asks students to show and explain why a particular concept holds true, in addition to giving formal proofs.

Much, then, depends on how the teacher thinks of mathematics, on the teacher's understanding of the discipline and its central concepts. Equally important, a teacher must understand how concepts can be explored in a classroom setting. A teacher like Kate knows different ways to begin and sustain the development and application of conceptual understanding, to open up simultaneously the content and the minds of her different learners. Kate is adept at identifying simple problems such as the banquet table that are immediately accessible based on familiar experience, engage students in algebraic thinking, support multiple solutions, and generate interesting variations to extend learning. From one such problem to the next she is helping students develop confidence and build algebraic understanding; their written accounts provide a record of their learning. To progress in this fashion requires knowing students well, knowing something about their preexisting understandings and their attitude toward mathematics learning, inquiring into their understanding in the moment, and having some ability to project, plan for, and continuously assess their long-term development as math learners. This is the point at which disciplinary and content knowledge become contextualized, and practice becomes personalized and equitable. Movement from subject matter knowledge to practicable classroom knowledge, however, is not simple, and standards, however valuable, do not readily help in converting one to the other.

Kate's Round demonstrates her integration of knowledge about subject, learners, and pedagogy. But in her class something more is at work as well. The focus, purpose, and tone are all one. As solemn as the Ten Commandments, Kate's "Shepardean Oath," posted near one of the doorways, frames up the culture for the students:

1. We shall show respect for ourselves and others at all times.
2. We will act as a team of mathematicians, discovering, discussing, and learning together.
3. We will regard the word *can't* as a swearword. We can achieve anything, we just may need a different approach or a little guidance.
4. We will never say the following phrase: "I am done." There is always something more to learn or someone else to help.

It has taken time to develop a mathematics learning community that values and validates thinking and that includes and supports everybody in the process of learning. That community, forming over a 2-year period with Kate, is given the time needed to mature. Here the school context comes into play. Not only does the structure of time help, but so does the enveloping school culture. What students experience with Kate is consistent with everything they experience at the school from their very first moments there. When they enter their science class, for example, they enter a room filled with artifacts of past student work and work in progress—with evidence of engaged minds—and a teacher who will also be with them for two years. In English class they will be treated as readers and writers from the first day. In history class they will begin to use primary sources in learning. Juniors and seniors will talk with them about taking advantage of the school. The partnership also comes into play, as Kate's students will see juniors and seniors going to and returning from university classes. And they will be supported by a student in the Master of Arts in Teaching program who is learning to teach under Kate's guidance. Kate herself is supported in her practice in the partnership, as she serves as both an instructor and Mentor Teacher in the Master of Arts in Teaching program and works closely with colleagues at the Hiatt Center. She hosts Rounds regularly for the MATs learning to teach; her students' learning gets frequent attention, her class becoming, in effect, a case study. The learning environment is rich and layered for the students and their teacher. Every nook and cranny of the culture proclaims that everyone is there to learn and that everyone can, and the expectation is that everyone will.

There is simply not a direct line from subject matter knowledge to standards to practice and student learning, in the way intended or implied by reform policy. Teaching and learning are much more multidimensional and contextual. When we ask what it takes to foster the learning that students experience in Kate's class, we need to take into account not only content, curriculum, and appropriate pedagogy, but also the coherence of purpose and practice and, likewise, the coherence of personalization and community in the learning culture of the classroom and school.

CHAPTER 5

Adelina Zaimi's Dilemma: Calculating the Slope of Learning

ADELINA ZAIMI WANTS her ninth-grade students at Claremont Academy to become algebraic thinkers as well as doers. In her view mathematics learning means both understanding and performance: being able to demonstrate the "why" as well as the "what" and "how" of mathematics. And to demonstrate the "why" students need to be able to think as if the symbols and numerical relationships were their own. The story of how she arrived at this conviction and the dilemma she must confront in her practice in order to stay true to it highlight the challenges entailed in establishing habits of learning that build students' confidence and competence as learners, as well as the transformative potential of collaboration within a partnership.

Adelina is only in her 2nd year as a teacher at Claremont Academy, her first teaching ninth-grade algebra. Last year she taught a numeracy class for eighth graders, a supplemental class established in Claremont's inaugural year to bolster support for underperforming students, comparable to a similar class at UPCS. Fourteen of these students are distributed in her current ninth-grade classes. She values her continued relationship with them and believes it has proven beneficial; most of the 14 have, in her estimation, progressed from the lowest to highest levels of performance over the past year and a half. For 2 years prior to Claremont she was a teacher's aide in a kindergarten class, a position that enabled her to learn English at a beginner's level. This was important for her, as she was a young mother of two recently arrived from Albania, via Italy, with little spoken English vocabulary beyond "thank you," a phrase she was wary of repeating too often.

TEACHING AGAINST THE GRAIN

Adelina's desire to be a mathematics teacher was born in elementary school in Albania, and she nurtured it in spite of constant concern about the correct methods for solving homework problems and anxiety that she would be asked to show her work publicly in class. Her school's philosophy of instruction adhered rigidly to the idea that students should grapple with assigned problems on their own. Students were distributed randomly in heterogeneous classes, and homework or problem-solving alliances between students were discouraged. Students might consult a teacher for help, but only if they had specific questions demonstrating serious engagement with the task beforehand. It was a system built on values of collective uniformity (one size fits all) and individual discipline, with learning resulting from individual effort rather than pedagogical design, and with development of a strong work ethic as a core goal.

Based on her formative learning experiences, one might expect Adelina's idea of teaching to lean toward an authoritarian model. Most teachers will acknowledge the lasting imprint of their own experience of classroom learning on their thinking as teachers. And even if they are determined to teach differently from how they were taught, they may have to work extraordinarily hard to attain the reflective understanding and make the paradigmatic changes necessary. Their challenge may be compounded if what they believe goes against the philosophical and cultural grain of their schools. Indeed, my colleagues in teacher preparation would agree that helping our students to clarify, exemplify, and sustain their "inner" practice—in particular, their beliefs about what constitutes good classroom teaching and learning—is a critical and integral dimension of our work. Our students, for example, might point to their use of "best practice" methods; yet, acting much like students in mathematics classes who perform an operation without understanding it, they actually expect their students to learn as they learned. They can easily mistake a change in method for a change in their support for individual learning. In other words, they might change the script of learning to some degree, but, absent probing and sometimes discomfiting analysis that penetrates the veneer of instruction, they will continue to write an overall narrative of learning in their classrooms that conforms to familiar beliefs and ways of acting on them.

A comparative study of mathematics teaching in Germany, Japan, and the United States, reported in *The Teaching Gap* (Stigler & Hiebert, 1999), suggests how deeply customary modes of teaching and learning can become ingrained.[1] The study found that teaching in each of the countries followed a recognizable pattern, albeit with some range of variation, and that different patterns resulted in qualitative differences in student learning as measured in the terms of international testing. The study characterized the different teaching protocols as "developing advanced procedures," "structured problem solving," and "learning terms and practicing procedures" (p. 27). The first two applied to Germany and Japan respectively. The latter model prevailed in the United States, which also had the poorest scores among the three countries in the comprehensive Third International Mathematics and Science Study (TIMSS); in fact, only 7 of the 41 nations involved in TIMSS scored lower than the United States. One of the most revealing findings of the study was the degree to which teachers in the United States followed the procedural approach in spite of believing that they were implementing the much different and widely respected reforms advocated by the National Council of Teachers of Mathematics, which, ironically, were evident much more in the teaching in Japan. There may have been changes in classroom scripts, but the overall narrative of learning, written deeply into the beliefs and expectations of the teachers, stayed more or less the same. This is not an unusual occurrence. Professional development initiatives often mistake the script for the narrative, assuming that the introduction of a new strategy—what some teachers regard skeptically as the ice cream flavor of the day—will lead to significant change in practice and student learning.

In order to change, teaching practice has to shift internally in terms of belief and understanding and not simply method; it has to move beyond reflexive to reflective action. A closer look at the difference between the procedural approach predominant in U.S. practice and the problem-solving approach followed in Japan helps make clear the challenge of doing so. The procedural approach emphasizes applying rules that have been explained and illustrated by the teacher to sets of problems. In contrast, the problem-solving approach consistently immerses students in developing and debating their own solutions to problems posed by the teacher. The first method is more one-dimensional than the other, emphasizing formulaic or operational performance, which requires a low level of understanding of the reasoning behind the solution. The structured problem-solving protocol followed in Japan is multidimensional, involving students in proposing, testing, and refining ideas, and aims for performance with understanding. Each reflects a very different set of beliefs about teaching and learning. In the one case, the teacher is the knowledge giver, the demonstrator of understanding, and students are the applicators of knowledge; in the other, the teacher is the strategic facilitator of understanding, and students are the codevelopers of it. Consequently, the relationship of student to subject matter is different in each case, as likewise the character of knowing that results. The procedural approach locates the source of knowledge entirely outside the student, keeping a broad intellectual distance between student and subject, as if getting close would be complicating, time-consuming, or inexpedient. In the problem-solving approach the student is closely connected. Procedural knowledge is bounded by the conditions under which procedures can be applied. The problem-solving approach values exploration of what does not work, as well as what does. Students are directly involved in mathematical reasoning, in formulating the "what," the "how," and the "why" of what they are doing.

As Stigler and Hiebert (1999) suggest, the difference between the procedural and problem-solving approaches is not a difference in method but a difference in cultural systems. Thus movement from one approach to another is tantamount to moving from one cultural system to another, implying changes in the beliefs, assumptions, and understandings that frame the daily assessment of student work and formulation of lessons. Adelina's conversion to a philosophy that values both understanding and performance is an example of how this fundamental change occurs. She was perhaps more prepared than others because of both lingering unease with how she was taught and, as an English language learner, her sensitivity to what it takes to assimilate and adapt to new symbols of communication. But she needed a precipitating agent, as well as a community of mutual support built on similar beliefs and commitments.

CONVERSION AND COLLABORATION

Adelina's moment of epiphany occurred unexpectedly when she participated in a session given by Kate Shepard of UPCS (featured in Chapter 4) to a group of teachers and Hiatt Center graduate students during an annual summer institute run by UPCS. The summer institute occurs in conjunction with a 3-week "academy" in which UPCS teachers introduce incoming seventh-grade students to the ways of learning at UPCS in the mornings and reflect on their work with teachers and MATs who have observed them in the afternoons. The seventh graders get exclusive attention in this rite of entrance into the UPCS learning community, and the adult participants gain insight into how UPCS teachers welcome them, engender trust, and help them see themselves as readers, writers, and thinkers. Kate demonstrated how she structures her lessons to support the development of algebraic thinking. Impressed by how Kate led her diverse students to understanding, Adelina embraced the philosophy immediately. And so she entered her first teaching assignment at Claremont confronting the question of how to convert her intellectual appreciation into exemplary day-to-day practice.

The journey from philosophical conviction to practice—in Adelina's case, from one culture of teaching and learning to another—is by no means straightforward, having its share of false starts, pauses, and recalculations; and, when traveled alone, it can be fraught with doubt. As helpful as curriculum principles and standards might be in establishing goals, they are silent in terms of formulating daily plans. Furthermore, there is the question of context—how to begin and continue with the particular students in the class and with whatever habits and attitudes toward learning they have acquired in the course of their schooling. What would enable Adelina to develop her practice, to maintain her course in the face of the inevitable uncertainties she would encounter?

In fulfilling her goal to become a teacher, Adelina did not automatically become enrolled in a dedicated system of support or collaboration intent on tackling the question of how to guide students into becoming mathematical thinkers and doers. Most teachers would welcome and appreciate such a system as a normal feature of their professional life. But it remains elusive for them, in spite of a history of support from studies such as *The Teaching Gap*, with scheduling and budgetary constraints perhaps the chief culprits discouraging institutionalization of practices such as mentoring and co-planning, which are important for professional learning.[2]

University-school partnerships have a unique capability to fill the "collaboration gap" endemic to the profession. One of the premises of our partnership is that through collaboration we fortify one another in examining and keeping our beliefs, values, vocational commitment, and practice on course. We endeavor to cultivate and sustain a professional learning community based on this premise. Part of the challenge is to learn how to learn together, to make common cause across institutional boundaries.

Several collaborative learning practices move us toward this goal. Rounds constitute one such practice and Curriculum Teams another, and whenever possible they are joined together. The Hiatt Center sponsors Curriculum Teams in the core academic disciplines (history, humanities, mathematics, and the physical and natural sciences) and, when external funding is expansive, in visual arts and foreign languages as well. The teams comprise faculty from the university, from both arts and sciences and education, and faculty from partner schools, elementary as well as secondary. Thus they span the spectrum from kindergarten to graduate school, and by design engender different kinds of cross-fertilization (between levels, schools, and types of expertise).

Several basic questions frame the work of the Curriculum Teams:

- How does one learn in the discipline? What are its habits of mind and practice—that is, what characterizes its "way of knowing"?
- What does it mean to understand and do something well in the discipline?
- What exemplifies authentic and powerful teaching and learning in the discipline at different levels of schooling in our particular context—that is, enables students to become engaged and increasingly capable readers, writers, thinkers, and doers in the discipline, consistent with curriculum goals and the overall goal of college readiness?

Summer institutes for students in the Master of Arts in Teaching program and for practicing teachers form yearly from the work of the teams. In addition, many of the teachers involved present their work at the Hiatt Center Best Practice Workshop—the highlight of an annual cycle of collaborative activity meant to engage members of the partnership community in developing, assessing, and exemplifying effective practice.

Adelina participates with Kate and other teachers on the Mathematics Curriculum Team. Having worked together on curriculum examples that promote understanding of mathematical concepts, team members this year decided to form subgroups based on curriculum standards close to their grade levels. Currently Adelina is working with several colleagues from Claremont to develop a set of exemplary plans focused on the concept of fractions. Kate, meanwhile, is serving half-time as a clinical professor at the Hiatt Center and continuing half-time teaching at UPCS. In this dual role she is an agent of cross-pollination and synergy, working at the intersection of practice, theory, and the working theories that form within each teacher, classroom, and school culture. Her dual role gives her an opportunity to visit Adelina's classroom, among others, and to attend Rounds. Even as she serves as consultant and coach during this formative period of Adelina's practice, however, their relationship moves toward collaboration. They teamed up, for example, to present at the annual Hiatt Center Best Practice Workshop, illustrating the development of conceptual mathematical understanding using examples of students' writing.

For more than a year Adelina has worked hard to construct appropriate tasks and lessons, drawing on suggestions from Kate and members of the Curriculum Team as well as an eclectic set of resources. Her effort falters, however, in the face of her students' struggle to understand linear equations, graphing, and the concept of slope. As I will illustrate, her dilemma shows the complexity of the decision making involved in matching philosophy and pedagogy, and the influence of context on the development of practice.

FINDING A PATH FROM CONCRETE PROBLEM SOLVING TO FORMAL KNOWLEDGE

Setting her goals by the state curriculum standard, Adelina wants students to be able to define the slope of a line, measure and describe it in numerical terms, and explain what it shows. If their understanding develops as she hopes, they will be able to determine, explain, and work with slope in several different ways: to explain the differences in slope between two or more different lines, to figure out the slope of a given line on a graph, to construct a line given its slope and the coordinates of a point on the line, to construct a set of lines with the same slope, to figure out the slope given a linear equation, and so on. In other words, they will be thoroughly familiar with slope and ways to express it, and facile with their understanding.

As a prelude to the investigation of slope she has introduced graphing, specifically the process of plotting points on a graph. One group of her students grasps the idea of graphing readily in the abstract, as they often do with mathematical concepts. Most, however, need and benefit from more concrete ways of entering into the subject. They build understanding by considering concrete problems that have some connection to what they already know in their everyday world and formulating their own ideas about them and how to represent them; and/or by working back and forth between concrete and formal symbolic representations. Their understanding does not follow a simple progression from demonstration to repeated application (the linear path of learning so often prescribed in textbooks). Students instead slowly warm up to their subject, exploring and revisiting it in different ways until they are at home with it. Two of these students are English language learners, whose challenges Adelina understands personally, yet still has to work hard to meet by finding the right mix of visual, nonverbal, and verbal ways to represent subject matter, and, equally, to earn their trust and facilitate their participation in the culture of learning she is striving to cultivate in the class.

When her students struggle with the traditional notation and symbols involved in calculating slope, Adelina decides that they need to revisit how a linear equation gets formed by constructing one for themselves. She tries Kate's version of the banquet table problem (described in Chapter 4). Most students respond to it gratifyingly well. Even her most disaffected and disconnected students write letters explaining how to calculate how many square tables will be needed, if placed end to end, to seat guests at the imagined King's banquet; most have sound reasoning based on the data. One student determines a rule from his data that Adelina has not heard before: to find out how many people can be seated, take the number of square tables available, add two to it, and then add on the number of tables again.

A follow-up activity called "Barbie Bungee," culled from online resources of the National Council of Teachers of Mathematics (n.d.), asks students to plot data they gather directly onto a graph, and to calculate the approximate slope. Students, in groups of four, predict how far a Barbie doll, with one rubber band attached to her feet and a second connected to the first, will fall in a bungee jump, and then measure the distance after the jump. They repeat the procedure, adding two rubber bands each time, tabulating and plotting the data—the number of rubber bands represented on the x-axis, the jump distance on the y-axis. To help make sense of the resultant "scatter plot," they draw a straight line through as many of the plotted points as possible, with the balance distributed equally above and below the line. They then must calculate how many rubber bands they would need if the bungee jump started from a height of 225 centimeters—about as high as they can go in the classroom. There is more than one way to do this calculation, with Adelina encouraging students to figure it out using their graphs, which might entail extrapolating their lines or using the slope, or both, although they can also look at their data tables. As with the banquet table problem, student engagement in all phases of the activity is strong.

Encouraged by student performance in these activities, Adelina gives students a conventional test of her own devising, based on what she thinks they should know. To show their understanding, students must write ordered pairs based on points plotted on a graph, graph linear equations, and calculate slope in different ways—using data pairs and graphs. The test uses formal language and symbols; there is no familiar concrete problem as context and no partnering. What is familiar is the traditional test format and foreignness of the language; many students react as if helpless ("I don't get this, Miss") and perform poorly. Adelina and I discuss at length what this might mean. We hypothesize that the format and language trigger a kind of learned helplessness or reminder of past test failure, shutting down students' intellectual effort and persistence.

There is also the question of making the formalized test questions intelligible and the students' problem-based knowledge useful to answering them. How might the connection between the problem-based and more generic and abstract formulations be strengthened? How might students be made to feel at home with the abstract language? What if, as part of the conclusion to the banquet table and bungee activities, Adelina had asked students to explain their data and graphs, orally and/or in writing, and then name their components using the common language of mathematics? Or what if students had to choose from among ordered pairs or equations the ones that most closely represented theirs? Or what if students had to formulate a new equation with different numbers and ordered pairs that would produce a graph with the same slope as theirs?

We also discuss some follow-up possibilities. With several classes, one in particular, Adelina is trying different strategies to improve the homework completion rate. Beyond talking with students (building relationships), making completion and effort part of the grading criteria, and calling parents, she is running class contests, with pizza, cake, or a trip to the neighborhood McDonald's the main lures. We consider a variation in which students in each class would set a teacher-approved class goal. Each day's data would have to be properly tabulated, labeled, and graphed, with a daily report on progress from a different pair of students, complete with a calculation of what will be needed to reach the goal.

Through these and other means, Adelina will continue regular, daily attention to the process of building formal knowledge of graphs and slope. She also feels pressure to move ahead in the curriculum to prepare students for their next big concept. What preoccupies her is how to make a good transition from the idea of function to the idea of systems of linear equations without compromising understanding and while providing a bridge between the concrete examples, which draw many of her students into an active process of understanding, and conventional mathematical expression. She decides to immerse students for several days in the algebraic thinking that underlies functions, using activity stations that will reinforce and build on their successful work on the banquet table problem.

BUILDING CONCEPTUAL UNDERSTANDING THROUGH STATIONS

Stations are a group of distinct activities organized around a central concept, each station involving students, individually or together, in thinking relevant to the concept. If constructed well, combining various approaches with distinct levels of challenge, station tasks can lead students into different and often more complex ways of thinking about a concept. By connecting what they learn at one station to the other stations, through discussion and writing, students in theory will develop good conceptual understanding, making conventional forms of the understanding more accessible. If constructed poorly, then the curriculum quickly succumbs to classroom entropy, the fear of many teachers, beginning teachers in particular. Adelina has seen Kate use stations very effectively; she understands the careful planning necessary to ensure that they are effective. She has approached her first try gingerly, planning slowly, waiting for a ripe moment in the curriculum, gauging her students' readiness for the greater independence that stations will allow them and also making sure that she herself is ready.

Drawing on the eclectic resources that she has begun to accumulate, Adelina prepares five stations. The activities will employ some of the conventional terms with which students have become familiar. Three of the station tasks depend on students interacting in pairs, using a game format, each having several levels of difficulty. Even though two tasks do not require interaction, Adelina encourages students to discuss their calculations with each other. Students will produce something tangible at each station as evidence of their thinking and will take a station posttest to determine what understanding has taken hold, and whether it can be expressed using conventional forms of notation. She anticipates that most students will need at least half a class period to complete and consolidate what they have learned at each station.

The stations Adelina has prepared may be summarized as follows:

- Station 1 requires that students interpret graphs of growth rates of children based on height and weight, familiar to most students from pediatricians' offices. Students answer a series of questions about the graphs and construct a graph of their own.
- Stations 2 and 3 concentrate on determining rules from ordered pairs, a variation on what students did with the banquet table problem. These two are in the form of a game. Students form pairs. In Station 2 one partner reads one "input" number and "output" number at a time while the other writes them in a double-column format and tries to determine the rule that results in the output number; in Station 3, one partner has to calculate the input and output numbers from a written rule while the other records them and tries to figure out the rule. The rules are handwritten on sets of colored, laminated cards, with each color indicating a level of difficulty. In each case students record the number of ordered pairs they need to determine a rule. This becomes their "score," with the goal to get as low a score as possible.
- Station 4 is a variation on Stations 2 and 3. One student places a plastic cube in front of the other student. The partner adds a number of different-colored cubes depending on what a given rule calls for. The first student must figure out the rule by considering what operation can be performed on one cube that results in the total number of cubes. They repeat this process, each time starting with a different number of cubes, until the first student determines the rule that results in each group of cubes.
- Station 5 returns students to ordered number pairs and graphing. Attached to one of the bulletin boards is a large piece of chart paper marked with a coordinate plane; pushpins allow students to identify points on the plane from ordered pairs formed by numbers selected randomly from small boxes labeled x and y attached to the board. Students connect two push pins with a length of yarn and determine the slope of the yarn line and the corresponding linear equation.

Adelina will assign students to stations based on how well they are likely to work together and their comparable levels of achievement thus far; she is wary that self-selected groups will be more social than productive in all but one or two of her classes, as not all students have developed a sense of group responsibility at this stage. She meets with Kate the afternoon before launching the stations to review her planning. Although she has done two Rounds before, she will not host a Round for this inaugural effort with stations, a sign of the risk she feels in putting her beliefs and hopes into action.

She and I decide to focus our attention on her academically and behaviorally most challenging class as the best litmus test for determining whether the stations are serving their purpose. The class is unusually small in size, with just 13 students enrolled, but rather uneven in terms of temperament, attendance, responsiveness, and progress. On each of two successive days the class numbers eleven; but two students who were present on the first day were suspended before the second, including one student whose behavior alternates between cooperative and confrontational, depending on the timing of Adelina's last conversation with his mother regarding his classroom work. Their places are taken by two other students on the second day, one a girl who attends intermittently and is often detached. An older boy, an 11th grader, performs well when he is engaged, which is infrequent. Another boy is socially removed, choosing to eat lunch in Adelina's room, where he feels comfortable, rather than with his peers in the intimate school cafeteria. There are two English language learners, both Hispanic girls, one very shy. There are also three students who were in Adelina's eighth-grade class last year; they attend readily, a sign of the rapport they have built with their teacher, which Adelina attributes to their history of working together—the 2-year relationship for which she has become an advocate. None of the students have severe learning disabilities; only one has an individual education plan. Apart from their particular personal needs and shared adolescent concerns and social pushes and pulls, what some of these students seem to have in common are habits of intellectual, emotional, and social disconnection from school work. They have become accustomed to failure and not trying or not caring, or both; the words and symbols of mathematics, especially if delivered in a teacher monologue—the medium becoming the message— arrive to them stillborn.

The start-up on the first day goes slowly, students restless as Adelina tries to explain the stations; one of the students who will later be assigned an in-school suspension must leave. We agree afterwards that shortening the introduction, assigning groups to the stations, and getting each group started in turn would have hastened their involvement. With nine students to begin the class—the English language learners are in their English as a Second Language class and arrive midway through—she concentrates on the first three stations. One student, declining to work with others, begins on the height and weight charts. The remaining students begin to work in pairs on determining rules involving simple addition and subtraction. Adelina explains and models the process involved for these two groups.

Once students begin playing the games, the dynamic of interest slowly changes. Conversation begins to percolate in the pairs, all of which are actively engaged, in some cases mimicking language that Adelina uses. Here is a short segment from one pair, Student A (a boy) and Student B (one of the Hispanic girls learning English):

> Student A: What do you do to get from that [an input number of 1] to that [an output number of -4]?
> Student B: Plus 3?
> Student A: It's a minus! What's the difference between them?
> Student B: 5—subtract by 5.

These students generate the following set of input/output pairs:

Input	Output
1	-4
2	-3
3	-2
4	-1
5	0
6	1

The class is close to ending at this point, and Student A concludes that Student B understands the rule when she says "subtract by 5." To be sure, I ask her what the output would be if the input were 10. She looks discomfited, and tries one or two answers that do not involve subtracting 5. I wonder if subtracting 5 is something she learned from Student A without fully understanding the meaning in English or its application as a rule to an input number. So I ask her how she determined that an input number of 6 has an output number of 1 and she readily responds. I repeat this question for several other inputs, including 7 and 8. It turns out that the pattern that is guiding her is in the Output column only. She adds 1 to the previous output number each time a number is added in the Input column; but jumping ahead to 10 is more problematic. It is unclear whether she is hampered by language constraints in applying the rule, or simply gravitates to the most visible number pattern. What is clear is that she is trying to figure out a pattern, trying to make sense of the numbers, and that she is doing this through interaction with a classmate, with its potential benefit to her English language development and sense of belonging in the class.

Adelina and I muse on the tentativeness of her steps into algebraic thinking and what it will take to solidify her progress. The next day she is paired with another girl in Station 4, and practices both using a rule and guessing the one that her partner is using. Adelina reminds her of what she learned in the banquet table problem. By the end of the class, with a little coaxing, she is able to state one or two rules softly through her shyness. The stations, in particular the process of figuring out rules and practicing them in a supportive peer context, seem to be providing her with the opportunity she needs to work her way into understanding, and, just as significant, for Adelina to understand her and personalize support for her learning.

The stations exemplify Adelina's broader effort to socialize her students into a way of learning that allows them to develop understanding in a frame of reference that makes sense to them. Her approach is calculated to help students develop self-affirming habits of learning and class community norms that include tolerance for the effort to figure out mathematical relationships, which, she hopes, will increase their patience in unpacking the meaning of conventional terms and, more broadly, their persistence in learning. But the process can be long and demanding, especially in her most challenging class, requiring considerable persistence and patience on Adelina's part. That is why it is important to have collaboration with colleagues like Kate in the university partnership, which acts as a leavening agent in her own development. And it is why it is so valuable to have a concerted effort in the school as a whole to make the learning culture she is trying to establish a common and seamless one for students in all of their classes.

CALCULATING THE SLOPE OF LEARNING

High expectations fall quickly without a scaffold of support for both teachers and students. Adelina has high expectations for her students, but they only become meaningful in terms of student engagement, understanding, and performance when students have the particular kinds of support and opportunity that they need; when, more broadly, they are immersed in a learning culture that socializes them into habits of learning that at once respect, affirm, and expand their understandings. Adelina must calculate at any given point the slope and trajectory of their learning and the kind of support that will enable all of them to move ahead. Call the process, in honor of her efforts described here, "calculating the slope of learning."

At this point in their academic development, the slope of learning for Adelina's students is steep (see Figure 5.1); it is a critical formative period for them, requiring a high level of carefully calibrated and personalized academic support. Only when they have developed habits of learning that build their confidence and capability as mathematical readers, writers, and thinkers will the incline of their learning begin to diminish, and will understanding and performance find a firm foothold. Such habits will form from a graduated series of lessons, such as the banquet table and the station activity, which give them accessible, varied, and recurring opportunities to trust,

Figure 5.1. Calculating the Slope of Student Learning

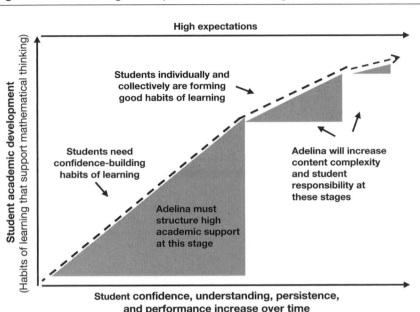

risk, explain, test, and develop their mathematical ideas, and which cumulatively ask for greater persistence and more mutual support. To the extent that students develop these habits, they will extend their intellectual commitment and willingness to confront more complex problems, and Adelina will be able to focus more attention on helping them to learn independently and collaboratively.

Scanning the walls of her classroom, I see tangible signs of Adelina's effort to define and develop the kind of support that students need. There is a scoreboard for the math homework contest. A Math Vocabulary Board is a record of concepts, such as variable expressions and exponents, that students have encountered since the beginning of the year. A Math Toolbox, which is a parallel to what good readers do, lists some of the thinking strategies that mathematical learners use. There are small blue booklets in which students record key ideas and concepts. There are more generic guidelines for group work and class procedures; she asks students to read them aloud prior to the station activity. Given the starting point of the personal journey that led her to Claremont, they are remarkable artifacts. At the same time, I know that Adelina has felt pressed—by time, intractable forms of student resistance, and the need to help her students replace old habits and expectations with new ones, all within a reorienting and redeveloping school culture.

Calculating the slope of students' learning and building a corresponding scaffold for their development is challenging and demanding work. Adelina will need all the help that Kate and the partnership can give to her as she adapts and develops her practice accordingly. Kate and the partnership will benefit too, as Adelina presents her work to her colleagues, and as they support each other through the curve of their own learning.

CHAPTER 6

Jody Bird and the Ecology of Curriculum and Teaching

JUDGING BY THE physical layout of the room alone, you might think Jody's classroom more elementary than secondary. One corner is framed by two bookcases overflowing with books, with a third bookcase set perpendicular to one of the walls, thus forming a study nook. Another corner has a teacher desk wedged into it, used by a graduate student from the Master of Arts in Teaching program. Yet another has a small desk with a computer—a workstation. The fourth hosts a second teacher desk, with a small laptop on it surrounded by an avalanche of papers. The walls in between the corners are crammed with posters and materials, some readily connectable to the biology curriculum: a model of a DNA double helix, posters with scientific information, samples of student work, an outline of curriculum standards (chemistry of life, genetics, evolution and biodiversity, structure and function of cells). A gray peeling beehive hovers high at the end of one wall. Two different-sized whiteboards, standing close beside each other as if parent and child, are on the wall between the two corridor doors. Large tables sit in the center of the room, with movable desks surrounding them. Large, sweeping curtains, cinched at the middle, frame two banks of windows that must have seemed impossibly tall to the elementary students who attended the school for more than a century before its reincarnation as UPCS.

If it appears disorderly, one misses the creative design in the way the classroom is set up. Jody's room reflects the multiple modes of learning more typical of elementary classrooms or teaching workshops—small-group projects or discussions can occur off to the side or within huddled groups of chairs; the center tables provide a location for demonstrations; there are opportunities for individual research or writing as well as whole-group activities. She has imposed variability and adaptability onto the squared space. As one gets to know Jody and the room, the irregularities reveal themselves to be signs of flexibility in approach amidst constancy of purpose.

Jody wants her ninth graders to learn to think and act as young scientists at the same time that they develop understanding of core biological

81

concepts. To meet this goal she knows that she has to meet as well the challenge of helping students mature as academic learners able to read for understanding, handle the dense Latinate language of biology, write clearly and accurately, appropriate various forms of data and evidence in writing, adopt to some degree the inquiring skepticism of the scientist with regard to knowledge of the physical world, collaborate, analyze, and represent understanding.

These three dimensions of purpose—thinking and acting as scientists (the disciplinary way of knowing), understanding central concepts (subject matter knowledge), and reading, writing, speaking, and representing (academic literacy development)—frame the learning in Jody's classroom. But which one is emphasized on a given day, or how they are each addressed in a single lesson and over time, depends on Jody's assessment of her students' academic development and capability (contextual and personal knowledge). Her knowledge of content, the scientific way of knowing, and literacy combine in a constant interplay with her understanding of her learners in determining what she will do and how the space will be used. Together they form an ecological model of curriculum and teaching (see Figure 6.1).

Jody calls on these different domains of teacher knowledge as she explains her purposes, rationale, and planned learning activities to several Master of Arts in Teaching students and a clinical faculty member during a pre-Round orientation. A teacher for 8 years at UPCS and a graduate of Clark University, Jody is hosting a series of Rounds for the group. Her teaching is a subject of study in their Science Way of Knowing course, which she helps instruct. If they expect the Round to be an infusion of uncomplicated wisdom, Jody jolts their confidence, announcing that she is having "a hard time" with her class. Typical of her candor, this is self-honesty with a mission and wonderfully instructive in terms of understanding the tenacious day-to-day pursuit of purpose in practice. We learn that by "hard time" she is referring not to behavioral issues (for which "hard time" is often a code word) but to the developmental transition of her students from UPCS eighth graders to ninth graders, from closely shepherded learners to more independently responsible ones ready for the academic rigor of Jody's class. All classes at UPCS are at an honors level beginning in ninth grade, to mark a new stage in college preparation, and the expectations for effort and performance are correspondingly high. Jody focuses the Round group first of all on context, in particular on her students' maturation as academic learners, situating the day's learning on a broad continuum of development. Her discussion reflects how her knowledge and assessment of her students enter into her teaching practice (the bottom circle and upper right, arrow in Figure 6.1).

Figure 6.1. An Ecological Model of Curriculum and Teaching

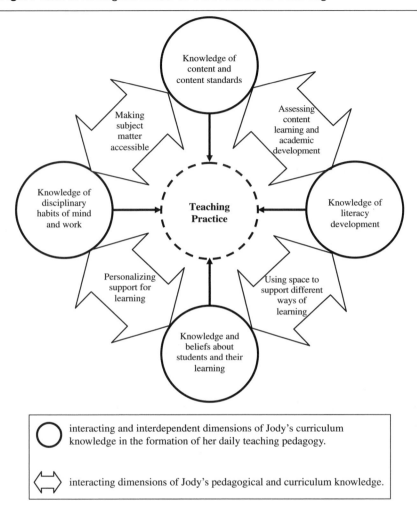

As she fills in the contextual background of the day's lesson, Jody high-lights two kinds of scaffolding, or forms of support for academic work, that she has constructed during the early period of the school year in an effort to build her students' capability to meet her expectations for content and disciplinary learning (the middle and upper circles in Figure 6.1). The first concerns science writing, about which she is "very purposeful"; the second, the use of literature circles to facilitate reading comprehension.

SCIENCE LEARNING AND THE WRITING WORKSHOP

Like other colleagues at UPCS, Jody is a strong advocate of writing across the curriculum, integrating both formal, discipline-specific writing and informal writing. To introduce students to lab report writing, she conducted a writing workshop. The *writing workshop* is a process, with teacher and/or peer support, for molding an idea and purpose into a credible and worthy written form. It generally involves moving back and forth between purpose and conception, format and draft, feedback and revision, and arriving at a shareable piece of work. Most teachers do not normally associate a writing workshop with a science classroom, and some might view the two as an odd interdisciplinary juxtaposition or an unnecessary and time-consuming digression, believing that students should arrive to science class ready to write. Indeed, writing workshops appear much more frequently in English language arts than science classrooms. The writing workshop, however, accommodates readily the writing necessary in other disciplines. For it is a matter of process not content, predicated on the seemingly self-evident but deceptively simple idea that good writing, including good lab report writing, requires practice, and that practice within a community of people likewise engaged enhances the experience for everyone. Let me suggest what this means.

Many students in school come to believe that writing is beyond them, an impenetrable ability that is granted only to a chosen few. Sadly, many also conclude, with disheartening certainty, that they have nothing valuable or valid to say, at least in terms of what counts in the academic world. To bridge the distance between this stance and some realization of the power of writing for themselves and, in turn, for their formal learning, students need the kind of support and opportunity provided by a writing workshop. They need well-traveled guidance to enter the forbidding maze of writing, to develop tolerance for its twists and turns, to appreciate its surprises, revelations, and satisfactions as well as its confusions and dead ends. This is true regardless of genre. The various genres of academic writing, such as a formal lab report, can be a form of black box for students, their norms and standards hidden by what appears to be a polished veneer of dense language. Opportunities to explore and study them, to become familiar with a genre's form, purposes, expectations, and basic characteristics, to practice working with words, ideas, and data within the genre, can help students develop a basic level of understanding and mastery over time. In workshop fashion students in Jody's class go through different stages of lab report development, drafting different pieces, getting peer and teacher feedback, revising, getting focused teacher help if needed (usually on an individual or small-group basis), and repeating the process periodically until their cumulative efforts begin to reflect the understanding of quality represented in her model and corresponding scoring guide. They develop academic literacy and competence; they become science writers.

Sometimes Jody offers a model lab report for the students to grade. One day she asks whether anyone gave her a grade of 100 on her lab report, which she had offered as a model in a previous class. She admonishes the presumption of excellence: "You shouldn't have. I had some mistakes in it." Jody works hard to cultivate a habit of critical examination in her class in tandem with an understanding of quality work consistent with the disciplinary norms of science. She often uses scoring guides and work examples and models as tools for teaching what constitutes good quality. This explicit induction into the academic way of knowing is particularly important for her students, almost all of whom come from families with limited school and college experience and who therefore do not see and practice academic habits of thinking, analyzing, and speaking in their home environments, unlike many middle-class children with one or more generation of college-goers in their families. By making criteria transparent, coconstructing criteria with students, and giving students practice in using criteria to assess Jody's mock models, actual models, and their own work, Jody helps her students develop an understanding of academic work. In this process she grafts elements of learning more typical of art studios or writing workshops—work is remolded and reshaped many times, neophytes learn from advanced practitioners as well as the teacher, and all receive feedback from "critical friends"—onto science learning. The classroom physical setup supports what is, in essence, a science workshop.

Jody complements practice in formal disciplinary writing with informal, low-stakes writing. For instance, students keep interactive notebooks in which they record their ideas in response to various prompts from their teacher and in the various forms she conjures up, such as brief student reflections or jokes based on a particular concept. Also known as writing to learn, informal writing is used as a tool both to facilitate thinking and to develop general facility in writing, emphasizing effort and thinking rather than content. One's best thinking in the moment (and of course it should be one's best), no matter how inchoate or rough-edged, is acceptable, and often diagrams or sketches can be included, expanding the possibilities for engaging students who, for one reason or another, lack verbal confidence. Informal writing can help students get reassuringly involved, bring their thoughts and ways of thinking trustingly into focus, build confidence while traveling the bridge to formal writing, and create a personal connection with subject matter. And students' informal writings invariably provide the teacher with important insights into their understanding, opening possibilities for building rapport and personalizing learning. In weaving writing and science learning together, Jody activates their symbiotic power—their mutual roles in developing understanding—as well as the power of the ecological approach of her teaching.

In parallel with writing, students learn to "read to learn," in part by using a small-group process designed to represent different aspects of what good readers in a discipline do. Jody has borrowed and adapted the idea of Literature Circles from a mentor who taught English.[1] In Literature Circles students take on various roles with different responsibilities, all of which involve them in examining, interrogating, or interacting with a text. The combined effort and sharing of individual students is meant to build a comprehensive understanding within the group of students. Students practice and rotate roles until, over time, they internalize and begin to apply good habits of reading more and more on their own. Jody informs the Round group that she adopted a literature circle approach to help students glean as much as possible from a *National Geographic* article titled "It's a Frog's Life," which students read as an example of how species interact with their environments. Literature circle roles, such as *Summarizer, Vocabulary Enricher,* and *Connector,* serve the purpose of helping students work together to make sense of the unfamiliar language and concepts of biology. In the process students pry open the interactive process between reader and text and make the development of the habits of good reading—and of learning— a shared enterprise.

By making the qualities of a good lab report explicit and giving students structured support for writing them and by integrating writing to learn and a collaborative effort to comprehend difficult texts, Jody combines literacy and disciplinary learning, makes academic capability transparent and developmental, builds her ninth-grade learning community, and strengthens the ecological web of their learning. As a biology teacher, she does not simply teach science content, but instead treats students as apprentices in the sophisticated world of science, helping them enter its discourse and acquire the habits of mind and work of its practitioners. She guides them in adopting a metacognitive view of their work, asking them not simply to know something in science, but also to be conscious of what scientific thinking entails and to develop understanding according to the norms and standards of the scientist. And she is doing this according to a developmental progression that makes sense for them, gauging and responding to their needs as academic learners, calibrating both the level of challenge and demand that they can meet and also the support she needs to give them.

TEACHER KNOWLEDGE AND PRACTICE

Jody's practice forms dynamically within the intersection of the domains of teacher knowledge in Figure 6.1. It is fed by her contextual knowledge and personal knowledge of students (bottom circle), informed by her continuous assessment of their development (upper right block arrow) and her knowledge of content, the way of knowing of science, and academic literacy (the remaining circles), and aligned with her understanding of the path toward college readiness that travels through ninth grade. Jody makes this integration of knowledge, judgment, and mission seem relatively routine; she speaks naturally and with characteristic animation and determination during the pre-Round. But it would be a mistake to view the integration reflected in her explanation of her practice as a natural and inexorable process. However well-meaning, another teacher, who is preoccupied with standards-based or test-driven instruction and treats the curriculum as territory that has to be covered by taking the most expeditious route—the "what" of instruction therefore overshadowing the "why," "how," and "for whom"—might bypass altogether the critical developmental and contextually important steps Jody discusses fluently.

The evolution of Jody's multidimensional thinking as a teacher is due in no small measure to her creative passion for students, for teaching, and for her subject matter, as well as her fearless self-scrutiny; she judges her teaching on the understanding and performance of her students. The professional environment at UPCS and her ecological niche in the partnership nourish the development of her teaching. Academic literacy development, for example, has seeped into the collegial pores of UPCS and the partnership over time, the process of connecting students' lives to subject matter through text and writing in multiple ways becoming part of its lifeblood. And the idea of developing students as scientists—or literary readers, historians, and mathematicians—is similarly embedded. Jody has had mentors and colleagues in English, history, and mathematics as keen as she to cross-fertilize practice that unites literacy and subject matter learning. As both a member and cochair of the Hiatt Center Science Curriculum Team, as well as assistant instructor in the Ways of Knowing in the Physical and Natural Sciences course, she immerses herself in thinking about and demonstrating best practice. Her practice both reflects and informs the learning culture of the school, as it does the collaborative learning goals and culture of the Hiatt partnership.

FROM CONCRETE EXAMPLE TO CONCEPTUAL UNDERSTANDING

Jody's effort to develop her students' academic capability up to the point of the Round links inextricably with her content learning goal for her students: to understand the big ideas of ecology and evolutionary history. She summarizes this on her Round sheet:

> Our class is in the midst of studying interactions among organisms and between organisms and their environment—ecology. The class has explored several types of species interactions and population dynamics. We've taken a closer look at the impact of human introduction of nonnative species to an ecosystem by watching the documentary *Cane Toads: An Unnatural History* and discussing Dutch elm disease during "storytime." The toad documentary was followed by a National Geographic reading, "It's a Frog's Life." . . . Given the complexity of the evolutionary history of native species, it is important that we revisit the impact of nonnative species during our evolution unit to complete students' understanding.

Jody designs her curriculum so that students will move from concrete example to conceptual understanding and back again, in dialectical fashion. By examining normal interactions between species and their environments in relation to disrupted ones, using examples of both native and nonnative species, students will encounter the conceptual power of ecology.

Jody's curricular path will travel through the concept of nutrient cycling and continue with two case studies, one asking students to use the data tools that scientists use, the other involving them more actively in the scientific process as they will gather data themselves, local data that will bring the idea of ecology more closely home. Her Round sheet charts out the path in more detail:

> [Today] students will uncover the ins and outs of nutrients cycling. . . . We will follow this learning activity with two case studies, *The Petition: A Global Warming Case Study* and *The Fish Kill Mystery*. The former explores how human activities contribute to greenhouse effects and global warming through the use of graphs and data the students must interpret. The latter focuses on the impact of land runoff and excess nutrients affecting aquatic communities, which will be used as a basis of study of the local Crystal Park pond. Students will analyze the water for various nutrients and determine sources of contamination. Both case studies are from the National Center for Case Study Teaching in Science [see http://ublb.buffalo.edu/libraries/projects/case/case.html]

and are adapted by me to meet the needs of my high school biology class.

Jody cites the state curriculum standard on her Round sheet to indicate what students should be able to do: "Explain how water, carbon, and nitrogen cycle between abiotic resources and organic matter in an ecosystem." She does not, however, address this content goal as an isolated bit of knowledge. True to her ecological understanding of classroom learning, it is connected to other content understandings and to her students' growth in literacy and scientific thinking.

Content standards are inert and impassive when it comes to a teacher's pedagogical decision making and a student's effort to learn them. They appear to fulfill the familiar curricular dictate to say what students should know and be able to do, yet they stand stern and bare, not clearly connected to larger disciplinary and educational goals, not to mention the complexities of classroom context. They rarely address disciplinary habits of mind, still less the relationship of content learning to students' lives. They neither take into account students' development as learners in the discipline at a given point in time, nor help a teacher plan how to teach them. Jody values them as guideposts, but she has to find the right place for them on the curricular path along which she is leading her students and incorporate them into the broader ecology of learning in her classroom. She not only wants the learning process to lead to meaningful conceptual understanding, but wants conceptual learning to be connective and cumulative.

Jody uses a weekly syllabus as a tool to make students aware of the flow of learning. Recent remarks by David Conley, who visited UPCS as part of his research on the alignment of high school and college learning, reinforced her resolve to keep students abreast of their program of study and responsibilities.[2] As she explains on her Round sheet, "The weekly syllabi not only serve a day-to-day function, but also provide a road map of their learning." On this Monday morning she notes her expectation that students will know what they are doing during the week and make connections between "today and before." The syllabus highlights the "learning goal/lesson" and homework for each day. Ninth grade is not too early to accustom them to the way content unfolds in a typical college class, a theme that has grown in prominence in the UPCS curriculum over the past 2–3 years, particularly in 11th and 12th grades.

As the best assurance of understanding, Jody plans to enable students to "uncover the ins and outs of nutrients cycling" themselves. As this is the first time that students will research something on their own, she structures a collaborative approach with a high level of individual accountability. In the Round lesson students will begin a "jigsaw" learning process, forming small "expert" groups, each charged with researching one of three bio-geochemical cycles (water, carbon, or nitrogen). As her instruction sheet informs them, they will be the "authority" on the material. One member from each expert group will be responsible for teaching students represent-ing the other two cycles in mixed expert groups, using visual presentation tools. Jody explains her strategic grouping: putting together two students interested in global warming in the carbon cycle group, taking account of students' strengths as presenters and visual artists, and considering the self-critical skills of different students as reflected in their evaluations of their own lab report write-ups.

Not once does Jody mention *ability*—that monolithic term, erected upon precarious judgment, too often used to categorize and sort students in class-rooms, schools, and teachers' minds, and to deflect responsibility for stu-dents' low performance. She clearly views students multidimensionally and is intent on integrating interests and learning strengths in the groups, as appropriate for the task at hand, so that they are complementary and mutu-ally reinforcing. She embraces their heterogeneity and diversity, endeavoring to form equitable and strong working groups. Apart from the clarity and appropriateness of the task and their readiness for it, the group alchemy is critical if students are to learn with and from each other. Perceptiveness, trial and error, and performance are Jody's chief guides in getting the group composition right.

Jody integrates presentation skill development and group work with content learning in the Round lesson. Everything is purposeful from the first moment of class. "As always we start on Monday with a . . . ," she begins and is greeted with a chorus of "syllabus." Jody asks what "TBA" (to be an-nounced) on the syllabus means and asks why there is an Al Gore quotation there. She points out that one of the students expressed interest in global warming—Al Gore's passion—and that there is an important connection to the day's learning, in the form of carbon cycles. Students silently affirm this sign of relevance.

Jody wants to model and critique presentation skills before launching the biogeochemical cycle research groups. As a prelude she asks students what they should be doing while listening to a presentation: As they are getting "input" from a presentation, they should be taking notes. Jody tells students that in preparing her presentation she has gone through the same process that she expects them to follow, including conducting a dry run and getting feedback from some 11th- and 12th-grade students. Then she begins, "Hello, my name is Jody Bird and I am a scientist." Her subject is phosphorous, an element needed by all living things, which is found in our teeth and bones. "This handout will help you." She reveals that the ultimate source of phosphorous is rocks and, after a dramatic pause clearly designed to capture attention, asks "How do we get it? Can anyone think how?" She refers to a diagram labeled "Phosphorous Cycle" on chart paper hung on one of the whiteboards at the front of the room that is designed to illustrate how phosphorous cycles through the ecosystem. The diagram lacks detail and depth, something she hopes students will notice and critique. She concludes by highlighting some of the impacts of human activity on the phosphorous cycle, including the problem of excessive amounts and concentrations resulting from overfertilized soil. Two students respond to her invitation to ask questions.

The follow-up focuses on Jody's mock presentation and criteria for a good presentation. One student suggests that Jody should have researched more on the water cycle and runoff that affects the phosphorous cycle. Jody takes this in good stride. Another says that she was "loud enough," and Jody asks why that is important. Jody says that she wants students to be critical—"that's how we get better." This is a culturally pivotal message because in Jody's classroom students learn in a culture of constructive assessment rather than narrow evaluation and judgment and develop understanding of their progress rather than simply receive grades. The rejected approach to assessment keeps the path of learning more or less in shadow, and knowledge of the academic ways of knowing and assessing more or less secret, as if the teacher were a member of a privileged and powerful priest caste, with tests and grades as rites of passage. The approach to assessment that Jody uses blazes a clear path toward "better" and strives to help students learn in a spirit of mutual support as they make their way, reflecting their teacher's belief in them and her expert guidance in an increasingly understood and valued effort by students to live up to her expectations.

Jody tries to elicit more observations: "What are some of the things you noticed I did?" Mulling the significance of the idea, one student mentions Jody's point that DNA would not be able to form without phosphorous. Jody fields students' thoughts about criteria for a good presentation and diagrams, writing them on the white board. Ideas such as "voice volume," "eye contact," "avoiding *um* and *like*," and "note cards" appear alongside "neat," "clear," and "organized." Jody observes that she did not read from her note cards but used them only as a reference. Typically, students generate more generic presentation concerns rather than content-related ones. Steering attention to content, Jody emphasizes the importance of addressing how humans affect the cycle. She stops there rather than address other aspects of content, such as what a good representation of the cycle might contain, sensing that she has reached a point of diminishing return in the discussion, and, as she explains in the post-Round reflection, she does not want to overwhelm students. Teacher and students together have developed a set of working criteria that will lead to a scoring guide. They are modest in scope; Jody balances student ownership against sophistication at this early stage in the classroom learning culture and intends to refine and elaborate them during students' preparation and actual presentations.

As she checks on newly formed student research groups, the challenge for Jody and students appears immediately. One student asks whether her group will need a poster for the presentation. Jody reminds her that "we talked about what makes a good presentation." It will take coaching and time for her students to develop a mental template of what this means. Jody directs students' attention to different resources, in particular some college text-books with which she wants them to become familiar over time—another sign of how the theme of college readiness enters her classroom. Students must finish work in their expert groups by giving themselves homework assignments that will help them prepare for their presentations. Thus Jody shifts as much responsibility for the work to them as they can handle and puts their thinking as much as possible at the center of the learning process. They must inform Jody of their self-assignments before exiting class.

OBSERVING AND PERSONALIZING

Jody has served as an assistant instructor in the Ways of Knowing in the Physical and Natural Sciences course for MAT students each fall for several years. Her own teaching serves as an entry and departure point for thinking about best practice—in all of its contextual complexity, as it unfolds in a particular classroom with a particular group of students, within the culture of UPCS. The post-Round discussion is part of a longer running conversation about best practice that engages Jody, colleagues at the Hiatt Center, and the graduate students.

Jody quickly assesses what went on in class, focusing on her main concerns: the development of presentation criteria, the performance of the expert research groups, the performance of particular students within the groups. She had hoped for more participation in the discussion of presentation criteria, more talk about human impact on the phosphorous cycle. These are signs that the students need more practice with critique and questioning, and help from her to understand quality work; the scoring rubric that she will introduce on the day of presentations will be an important tool in this respect. She had anticipated these topics in one of her questions on the Round sheet: "Is there evidence in the students' dialogue that they are taking ownership over the criteria of their presentations? If so, please write down your evidence." She invites observations: "It would be helpful to me to hear what you noticed in groups . . . what about student conversations?"

Characteristically, Jody focuses attention on particular students, gathering vital information to inform her ways of working with them. Pairing two particular boys "worked like a charm." Jody notes her elevated expectations for these boys and their three-person group, the higher level of challenge that she has set for them. They are the only group working on the water cycle, and the only one that will present to the whole class. The four other groups, two each working on the nitrogen and carbon cycles, will be re-formed for purposes of presentation, with all students responsible for talking about some aspect of what they have learned. Jody raises a concern about one girl's academic development. On the one hand, she produced a lab report in the writing workshop that showed a promising understanding of what it should contain. But she is "conversationally" reserved, making it difficult to know her degree of intellectual engagement in group work. "Who observed her in her group? Is she playing that 'I-don't-get-it' card?" Jody is alert for feigning and excuse making. Her graduate teaching intern offers that the two other members of this girl's group seemed to be carrying the workload. That leads to consideration of another of Jody's Round questions: "Would students have stayed more on task in their groups if they had had assigned roles? What roles would you have given them?" There is a short discussion on how roles can stifle participation in some instances and whether roles might have been limiting in this case, given the small size of the three-person expert groups. Regarding the student in question, Jody says that both she and the teaching intern need to "keep an eye out for her understanding" the next day.

Observations generated through the Round feed Jody's determination to personalize instruction, the constant process of inquiring into students' learning so as to determine what might help them go further. The questions that percolate steadily beneath the surface of her visible practice come briefly to light: How do I adjust group responsibilities and guidelines? What do I look for to gauge students' engagement and understanding? What support might help a particular student most? When in her development is a student ripe for challenge and how do I provide it in the context of the overall class learning goals? How do I make up for the miscalculations or shortcomings of the day? How do I mobilize the interdependent elements of the ecology of learning for the benefit of all?

PRACTICE INVISIBLE TO THE EYE

"What is essential," the fox said to the little prince in Saint-Exupéry's (1971) classic, "is invisible to the eye" (p. 87). Jody's invisible practice—the beliefs, empathy, understandings, purposes, and habits of mind of a teacher—becomes vivid in the Round discussion. She demonstrates how an experienced and dedicated teacher thinks about and pursues purpose in practice on a daily basis. Viewing it casually and in isolation, one might not appreciate the lesson as one of the strategic small steps necessary for enacting a larger vision. Its power lies in the ecology of learning at work, in the transparency and equitability of the learning process, in how it fits into the developmental picture for her students that Jody holds in her mind's eye, in the effort to align students' experience with the culture and mission of their school.

Classroom teaching is a dynamic and contextual process, a reflective effort to engage students, who are diverse in various and wonderful ways, in mindful interaction with meaningful subject matter, in a particular social and cultural space, and in relation to a set of larger disciplinary, educational, and democratic purposes. Jody and the Round group participate in one magnified episode of this process, a momentary reflective community forms, and the dynamic is honored in all of its personality and challenge, and inherent faith and hope.

CHAPTER 7

Putting Inquiry Into Practice: Chris Rea and Investigating Harmonic Motion

WHEN YOU ENTER Room 309, two things are apt to strike you right away. First, this is a classroom with floor-to-ceiling walls, an anomaly at South High with its open space design. Second, duckpin bowling balls are hanging from the ceiling on blue cords, one within reach of each cluster of four desks. Even if you view physics as impenetrable, you cannot help but be intrigued. And this is precisely what Chris Rea, graduate student, hopes for: "I am conscious of creating a physical space for learning that invites the curiosity of students."[1]

Chris is leading a Round. The pre-Round conversation is held in the library prior to the start of class. Two education faculty members, a teacher who acts as a liaison in the partnership with South High, a graduate student teaching at University Park Campus School, and the physics teacher with whom Chris works (his Mentor Teacher) are in attendance. Two other graduate students and another Mentor Teacher will join the group during the course of the Round.

LOCATING RESPONSIBILITY FOR LEARNING

Chris is typically thorough in his preparation and explanation of the Round. Characterizing it as "Discovering Harmonic Motion" on his Round sheet, he signals his intention to support his students in developing their own understanding of the behavior of repeated motion. As he puts it, "The lesson is . . . inquiry- and research-based; the vast majority of responsibility for learning has been placed on students, for better or for worse."

In addition to his philosophy of investigative learning and student responsibility, Chris's statement discloses his sense of risk and uncertainty. Although it is March, and he has been teaching the class since the beginning of October, he is not entirely sure whether the students are ready for the degree of self-direction it will require. This puts him in the position of having to relinquish a certain measure of direct control over the content and of being prepared for the possibility that students will flounder, if not take advantage of a teacher who uncharacteristically retreats from the foreground of action. Chris acknowledges that "teachers, like me, are often terrified to place the responsibility for learning in the hands of students. We may be terrified for good reason. Sometimes when we try this, classes descend into chaos, learning stagnates, and productivity in the room drops to nearly zero." This is only one of many challenges he must meet in developing his practice in accord with a philosophy of inquiry.

Most teachers will recognize the dilemma of teacher control and direction versus student self-direction. Like Chris, they will have a healthy worry about the uncertainties involved in giving students a more central role in producing knowledge in the classroom. Some will view the problem primarily as one of behavior management, and see teacher direction and a tightly reined curriculum as essential for classroom order. A few might frame it in terms of the political dimension of teaching and civic goals. They consider the process of learning content as inseparable from the process of learning to think and act democratically; they strive to make learning a highly participatory activity.

Many teachers resolve the dilemma in their interpretation of mandated curriculum standards. Standards were introduced in Massachusetts, as elsewhere, as a central piece of the equity puzzle: to level the field of opportunity for all students, increase rigor in the curriculum, and promote minimally acceptable levels of achievement. But, as it turns out, equity in classrooms and schools does not necessarily follow from equality in the curriculum; nor does powerful learning necessarily result. So much depends on what the standards are, how many of them there are, whether they are subjected to a timeline, to what purposes they are harnessed in the overall curriculum, how the content and academic discipline involved are represented, and what theories of learning and practice are followed in the effort to fulfill them. Even more fundamentally, teachers have to understand them and believe, along with their students, that everyone can achieve them. But it is not a simple matter to attain this state of mind for many reasons, not least because institutional practices often say otherwise, as when students are placed in ability groups or tracks that suggest that the possibility of achievement may be greater for some than for others, a message that students internalize all too readily.

CHALLENGES IN CONSTRUCTING A CLASSROOM INVESTIGATION

Consulting the state curriculum framework in science and technology/engineering (Massachusetts Department of Elementary and Secondary Education, 2006), Chris will find ideas congenial to his inquiry-based approach. The overview and guiding principles stress that inquiry, investigation, experimentation, and problem solving—and the habits of mind they entail—are central features of the discipline of science and accordingly should be core components of science learning in the classroom. The framework even goes so far as to point out that students learning under the influence of this way of knowing will commonly experience "puzzlement and uncertainty" and will need time and opportunity to examine their ideas, as well as to "collect evidence, make inferences and predictions, and discuss their findings" in order to achieve understanding (p. 11). Following this encapsulation of the characteristics of science learning, the actual curriculum standards appear. The standards are organized by science domain (earth and space science, life science, the physical sciences, and technology/engineering) and grade level. They are statements of what should be learned. The most relevant for Chris's purposes indicate that students should know the measurable properties of waves, such as velocity and frequency, and the relationships among them. There are no examples, however, of an inquiry-based learning plan based on these standards. So Chris is on his own in fashioning a powerful classroom investigation.

Constructing a classroom investigation that truly represents a scientific process of inquiry and leads to understanding of an important concept is not a simple matter. In the case of Chris's Round, not only does it require an understanding of both inquiry and harmonic motion and its many manifestations and variations, but this understanding has to be translated into a set of investigatory tasks, and these tasks, in turn, must be possible to conduct in a classroom setting. Furthermore, Chris needs to consider the state of his students' capability to conduct an investigation. As a result of that assessment and in order to forestall, as he puts it, classroom chaos, he must decide what further development they need and how to support it. These considerations are all prior to deciding what evidence will reveal students' understandings, determining when and how to collect it, and settling the details of material and organization. Matters are further complicated as Chris considers what he knows about each student in the class and what he needs to take into account to ensure that each is engaged. Looking back, Chris reflects that he "relied much more heavily on the inquiry activity itself to engage students, rather than on specific thinking about how to engage particular individuals. Inquiry is fun and authentic and thus engaging by nature, at least relative to reading a textbook or listening to a lecture. I played on this to engage my students in learning, and then focused my efforts on addressing individuals during the lesson. Still, it was my deep familiarity with the activity that enabled me to support individuals, which suggests that making curriculum one's own may be important to powerful teaching and learning." Personalizing the learning process may be his biggest challenge. His "deep familiarity" is an asset in meeting this challenge because he is able to think of more than one way to connect a particular student's thinking with subject matter and the learning process.

As clean and straightforward as it appears, the path from standards to effective teaching practice and student understanding is not a direct line, but travels through layers of institutional and social context. In fact, if standards are treated narrowly or simplistically, they may prove inimical to learning. Unfortunately, this treatment occurs more often than we would hope, depending on a teacher's knowledge and experience and/or the pressure teachers and schools feel to prepare students for corresponding tests. Under pressure, many teachers feel compelled to deliver the content didactically and direct classroom action with authoritarian resolve. The imposition of state or district timelines—so much has to be covered in so much time—reinforces this tendency. Chris writes: "I myself struggled with the pace of inquiry in my own class, fearing that I was not covering standards quickly enough." But because there is no state exam in physics, he felt "freedom to delve deeply into the slower pace . . . [and] far richer realm . . . of inquiry teaching."

Curriculum principles such as inquiry get abandoned quickly in test-pressured environments. And tolerance for "puzzlement and uncertainty" withers along with them; after all, as Chris points out, state tests are "typically not inquiry-based," and do not "allow for 'puzzlement and uncertainty' in scoring." In these moments of a teacher's interpretation and translation of standards to practice, reform becomes paradoxical. Teaching becomes increasingly conservative and constrained, and equity and the quality and extent of learning suffer. In its most reduced form, standards-based teaching means giving students pieces of knowledge to swallow as if they were preparation pills for the impending test. Students are deprived of the real food of learning when listening and memorizing or following formulaic recipes of writing and reading rather than thinking from a desire to do so, interacting inquisitively with a provocative text, learning to write by writing about something that matters, expressing and testing their own ideas, solving an engagingly perplexing problem, or in one way or another figuring out something meaningful about themselves, each other, and the world they share.

That standards and testing do not necessarily lead to good teaching and learning may be explained best by the fact that good teaching is a complex and contextual act. Chris needs to be at once proactive, responsive, and adaptive; he is an architect of activity, a guardian of high expectations, an organizer of a small community, and a clinical observer who caringly understands and responds to his students' progress and needs. His practice is an intricate interplay of content and pedagogy, of knowledge of subject matter and its possibilities, and knowledge of students and their personal and collective development as science learners. Standards—in their static and lifeless form, disconnected from disciplinary principles and learning theory—tend to straighten and smooth out teaching's edges and true personality. Good teaching can abide and even thrive with good standards, particularly in light of the democratic purpose to educate all well; but it also defies standardization in timing or format. Regimentation and simplification sap the curriculum of its vitality, homogenize students, and depersonalize the classroom, consequently diminishing teaching's demands and depriving it of its mind, its democratic heart, and its soul.

The school environment and the structure of support for Chris's development as a beginning teacher also affect his effort to enact an inquiry-based way of knowing. On the one hand, he felt "continually supported" in his program in terms of philosophy of learning and mentoring. Nonetheless, looking back, he writes, "I struggled day to day to integrate my philosophy and practice in the classroom." He and his peer team, as well as their students, had to navigate crosscurrents of philosophy and approach in the culture of belief and practice in their school setting. Inquiry was not a natural or customary learning process for many of his students, and he had to socialize them into what is taken for granted in the academic world. Furthermore, it is not particularly easy, especially for a beginning teacher, to conform practice to conviction. Integrating the two is usually a matter of fits and starts. Chris must learn not only how to translate belief, theory, and purpose into practice, but also how to interpret and learn from practicing, mainly from the experience of the learners themselves. This process is much more than a straight line from theory or research or curriculum standards to application. It is much more dialectical and recursive, much more personal and contextual. And it is daunting for beginning teachers like Chris who are learning to meet the challenge of planning for each class, each day, and each week.

Depending on one's experience of practice, and the environment and culture of the school, one's sense of belief and purpose itself can be put in jeopardy. In turn, the challenges for those of us acting as mentors of Chris and his peers in the program, and in partnership with the school, are manifold. We must try to tailor teaching responsibility and individual support to their pace of development, and create room for daily and weekly premeditation and reflection in the midst of real teaching. We must foster an experience of supported growth and community rather than debilitating survival, isolation, and constrained, defensive teaching.

SUPPORT FOR TEACHER AND STUDENTS

A number of specific conditions help build a positive context for Chris's effort to implement an inquiry-based approach that will immerse his students in scientific thinking and investigation. His rapport with his students and the culture of learning he has developed with them figure critically. Chris makes certain assumptions about his students' readiness and willingness that would have been premature in October, when he first began to work with them. He is also enmeshed in a network of support and shared experience, as intended in the design of the program. In curriculum planning sessions with his peers Chris has some opportunity to debate how to open up the content so as to engage his students intellectually and foster genuine scientific investigation and thinking; he considers these forums most valuable in terms of "frank and critical discussions of pedagogy."

Rounds bring this community of learning and practice directly into his classroom. Perhaps more than any other aspect of his Master of Arts in Teaching program, Rounds lead him and his peers to experience the bonds of their mutual vulnerability and personal hopes as teachers, as well as the power they have to learn from and with each other, so important for their growth and the growth of the profession. Many teachers might find the idea of inviting people into their classrooms to make observations about their students' learning as an intimidating act, judging by the small number of teachers who volunteer to do Rounds upon first hearing about them. But Chris has told friends "that if I ever open a school, I will strive to make the Rounds process part of the learning that goes on for teachers . . . [because] it did help teachers open their practice to the view of others, force teachers to reflect on their teaching in powerful ways, provide a forum for sharing good practice, and worked powerfully to build a culture of support and care among MATs."

Chris prepares the investigation-centered approach he will use in his Round with assurance of support from the Round group. He is also taking a calculated risk with his students, as he has worked over time to build their capacity for investigating physical phenomena. He documented an early moment in their evolution as investigators in a videotape used for a "Teaching and Learning" seminar at Clark University in November, soon after he became their teacher. As he explains in his Round sheet to introduce the videotaped class, students in small groups are attempting to "derive an equation of motion" from a graph of data. This challenge culminates a path of learning that began with a discussion of the meaning of the equation $a = (v_f - v_i)/t$. Drawing on their experience with roller coasters, the class decided that the equation means "acceleration is change in velocity per certain amount of time." Chris wanted them to grapple with the mathematical expression of an experience most could verbalize without using numbers: "By helping them describe the motion of a roller coaster to derive an equation I aim to draw [a] direct link between understanding students already possess and the abstract form of a mathematical expression they do not understand at first glance, but that they actually can understand quite readily."

Arguably, he might have done well to introduce the equation at a later point in his students' study of speed and acceleration; but now at least they have a working definition to match up with a new experience analogous to the roller coaster. They proceed to collect and analyze data from observations of bowling balls released from the tops of handicap-access ramps in the hallways of the school, the source of the graphs they try to translate in mathematical terms. For Chris the path from observation to mathematical description is true to how knowledge in physics develops and gets expressed, and thus immerses students directly in the discipline. But Chris is using more than a discipline-based pedagogy. Context matters. He is conscious of the development of his students as learners, of the challenges posed for them in this joint engagement of their hands and minds in concert with others. And he is concerned about it.

As the class unfolds on videotape, Chris circulates from group to group, listening to discussions, probing for ideas, asking questions, making observations. Once he pauses to invite the class to "check out" the work of one of the groups; some students peer over, but others are too absorbed in their own group work or uninterested to do so, and it is unclear whether Chris thinks there is a lesson there that everyone should see.

On several other occasions, at a certain point in their thinking, he leaves a group with the message that he will let them figure it out from here—his effort to give them no more support than what they need to keep on their own path to understanding.

Chris superimposes questions onto the videotape about the impact of his interaction with the groups; for instance, "Am I engaging anyone besides Esther? Am I asking too many questions? Is frustration moving students to learning or is it pushing them away?" Some students are more involved than others, and Chris struggles with how to engage them. By the end of class chart papers begin to fill with drawings, graphs, and equations accompanied by brief written explanations. Afterwards they hang along the walls in testimony to days filled with measuring, timing, recording, and learning the mathematical language of physics. All of the groups derive appropriate equations from the data.

In this manner Chris accustoms his students to the habits of mind and work involved in scientific investigation, and learns what is entailed in doing so. He and the class have built rapport in this process during the months leading up to the current Round on harmonic motion. In this new study he is relying on the precious and fragile sense of trust that has grown on the part of the students, the psychological foothold they need along the path to bringing themselves fully to learning, to venture expressing and testing their own ideas, to risk being wrong.

The class we will view for Chris's Round is not quite as freeform as he conveys in the background section of his Round sheet. In fact, he has worked hard to create conditions that will support active engagement and generate ideas about motion that students can test and discuss. As he notes in the focus section of the Round sheet, "Despite the open-ended nature of the inquiry . . . the lesson *is* highly structured." What might appear to an untutored observer as a bewildering and uncertain process in actuality is guided by a carefully developed task, the appropriateness of the phenomena to both task and purpose, the strategic grouping of students, and Chris's effort to interject observations and questions that will focus and sharpen thinking. Chris's guide sheet for his students is indicative. It asks for very specific observations and conclusions about the physical phenomena. As Chris comments, "Inquiry looks messy, but requires elaborate planning and careful craft, much more so than traditional teacher-centered, lecture-style teaching. As a result, it is also highly time-consuming!"

STRUCTURING INQUIRY

The pre-Round conversation separates out the content and pedagogy interwoven in the lesson. Like his students, the participants in Chris's Round represent different perspectives, and not all are knowledgeable in the ways of harmonic motion. Chris explains the basic phenomena that students will investigate using two or three different "harmonic motion devices," such as "a pendulum hanging from the ceiling [the bowling balls], a mass on a spring, or even a chain of rubber bands tied together to make a vibrating string." Members of the Round group discuss briefly the regularities of motion represented by pendulums, familiarizing themselves with what students likely will be thinking about; unfortunately, time does not permit them to get more firsthand acquaintance with pendulums prior to the class.

Turning to curricular philosophy, Chris emphasizes the importance of connectivity. As he puts it eloquently in his Round sheet, "throughout the year I try as much as possible to avoid the compartmentalization and isolation of concepts, preferring instead to build concepts on previous concepts and, as much as possible, relate ideas, understandings and phenomena to each other." He hopes that the investigation of harmonic motion prepares students for an impending study of waves. We discuss briefly how one relates to and can flow into the other.

Attention shifts from content and curriculum design to pedagogy and the social context of this day's learning. Chris structures the inquiry learning process in several distinct stages. In what is essentially an observation and interrogation stage, students watch harmonic motion and endeavor to describe its regularities, with questions on Chris's guide sheet as prompts. Subsequently they must discuss and agree on how to describe the motion and relationships between its parts—for example, what happens to each back-and-forth swing of a pendulum in relation to time, the starting point of the swing, and/or the weight attached to it—and how to put their understanding in mathematical form. Finally, they move from observation and evidence-based discussion to representation and explanation. In this concluding phase, they develop a poster that illustrates the motion and its parts, summarize their understanding of the motion in writing, and describe it mathematically.

Chris clearly places strong emphasis in this lesson on knowledge development as an interactive process. Students must work together in formulating and presenting their ideas. In theory this means they will be involved in a complicated process of clarifying and sharpening observations for each other, confirming or qualifying what each other sees, raising questions, doubling back to check ideas, and testing whether their hunches and projections about what happens when circumstances—such as the length of the string or the extent of the swing—are changed.

Feeling pressed by a full curriculum timed to a standardized test, a teacher might view this way of learning as inefficient and messy. For Chris, however, the inefficiency and messiness are one measure of authenticity, a sign of students engaged unself-consciously in real thinking rather than in an expeditious search for an answer. If it goes according to plan, their complex interaction with the phenomenon and with each other—and the final agreed-upon expression of ideas in verbal, visual, and mathematical form—will lead to some depth and confidence in their understanding.

Philosopher David Hawkins (1974), inspired by John Dewey, described this kind of learning as "living in trees" (p. 173). The tree is his metaphor for what happens when a learner engages with subject matter in exploratory and intentional ways, its many branches and their intertwining pathways representing the searching, choice making, wondering, connecting processes of individual learning, as compared to the straight-ahead pathways implied in the logical ordering of formal knowledge in textbooks and school curricula. In this experience of learning, students develop maps of subject matter terrain themselves, rather than attempt to read a set of directions written by someone else, which usually have a single, direct route of travel in mind.

INQUIRY AS MAPMAKING

From the standpoint of learning, as Hawkins (1974) contends, when students follow a single path they lose the benefits that come from having had to explore and then choose one way over another. There is a great difference whether one is a path follower or a pathfinder, whether one walks along with blind faith or along a way that makes sense after some surveying of the land, after acquiring some orientation and familiarity with place. In the first instance the learner must adapt to a predetermined route; in the other, the route forms in concert with the learner's thinking. Of course, guidance from someone who knows the terrain—the teacher—is important; in particular, someone who knows good starting points, the choices possible in the face of an impasse, promising directions, and the views afforded from one prominence or another, and who can introduce them as needed to help a student along. Hawkins suggests that powerful teaching and curriculum have this embracing view and provide for this approach to learning; that learners who have an opportunity to map the topography of subject matter are in a ready position to understand, if not formulate for themselves, more formal knowledge. To the extent that every student can find some congenial point of departure and receives strategic support along the way, this approach is not only potentially engaging but also personalized and equitable, for personalization is the cornerstone of equitable teaching.

As powerful as they can be, mapmaking and pathfinding are not simple to achieve in a classroom, and small groups can be as much a weak as a strong agent in the process. As anyone who has participated in them knows, a whole host of unintended consequences can occur: Individuals can be left behind, data gathering derailed by someone impatient with the process, minority views tabled, answers valued over understanding. To safeguard against them, Chris reluctantly refers students in his instructions for their group posters to their books and the formalized knowledge they provide as a potential help—the first time he has done so in the class. He also has constructed a partial road map for them in the form of his guide sheet questions. In addition, he has formed groups based on the likelihood that they will follow the structured inquiry plan faithfully. Though he wants students to think their own way to new understanding, Chris is clearly hedging his bets, not wanting to let them—or himself at this early stage in his development as a teacher—venture too far without a strong tether.

Deciding whether to form groups, and how to form and develop them so that their members respect each other and think and work well together, is a matter of strategy and knowing students well: their personalities and academic and social strengths. "There is no sense," Chris emphasizes, "in giving individual work to a group; as with all learning, the task must be authentic to be powerful, and thus group work must truly require a group to complete it to be successful." For Chris, the question is also bound up with his effort to ensure equitable opportunity and support for students, to enact an equitable pedagogy.

Grouping by perceived ability or performance is the norm at South High, with exceptions resulting from planned heterogeneity in 9th- and 10th-grade classes of the Information Technology Academy, and otherwise from limited scheduling options (as addressed in Chapters 2 and 9). Chris's class is one of the scheduling exceptions. Comprising 11th and 12th graders who take physics as a science elective, his students are diverse academically as well as socially. He describes the class as fairly even in terms of boys and girls, having a higher concentration of English language learners than many other classes, and including both high- and low-achieving students. He takes these characteristics into account in his planning by grouping students whose personalities and strengths seem complementary and who are most likely to be peer teachers for each other.

Just before the members of the Round group enter this class on harmonic motion, we review Chris's Round questions, the framework of inquiry into his practice and student learning that he gives us. They reflect his chief concerns and goals:

I am interested in the inclusiveness and equity of the learning community in the classroom. Watch for disengaged students (and try to engage them if you are so inclined!) and also keep an eye out for highly engaged students. Watch especially for peer instruction, for group problem solving, and for student-driven learning. I am always aiming for ways to allow students to genuinely construct their own understanding, and also aim to create as many informal peer teachers in the classroom as possible. Given this, my biggest question is, are students learning from each other and individually in equal and deep ways? Do they really understand something about the way the universe works through their work, or do they only reinforce misconceptions? In short, are my methods working? . . . To what extent are language barriers an obstacle for learning? Are students mostly able to work around and through these barriers, or do language barriers hinder learning in large ways? What obstacles do students face that disengage them or turn them off from learning? This lesson and unit depend heavily on vocabulary. I have given no explicit instruction on this vocabulary, however. To what extent are students learning vocabulary and becoming comfortable using it?

A bell signals the start of class, the cue for Chris to announce "bell work." He crisply tells students that we will "get right into our work," reinforcing a routine meant to facilitate a quick transition to learning. He asks students to talk to their neighbors about their findings thus far, and discussion ensues. Following the questions on the guide sheet, several students consider how to figure out how often a pendulum swings from one point to another and back again in the space of a second. As Chris had hoped, they use the term *cycle* to refer to this forward-and-back swing motion and *frequency* to refer to the number of times it occurs per second.

When he gathers their attention as a whole class, he asks for examples of what students have figured out. One group announces their calculation for cycles per second. Chris asks, "How did you do it?" After one student describes the group's method, he responds, "That's completely the right track." The student who offers the explanation is one who scowled at an attempt at humor by Chris as she struggled with a problem on the videotaped class from months ago, causing some momentary soul-searching on Chris's part. But clearly her thinking is valued in the class, and she is happily contributing.

The latter part of the class is devoted to the preparation of posters depicting harmonic motion and explaining it with diagrams, words, and mathematical expressions. The posters help students make sense of the data they accumulate and move toward general descriptions of the phenomena. Looking at one group's diagram, of a pendulum, Chris encourages them: "Describe it [in writing] . . . tell me what you are thinking." He concludes the class by asking students for an "exit slip" on which they are to draw one of the harmonic motion objects they have studied and show him "the forces acting on it." By asking for an illustration instead of a written description, Chris hopes to make it possible for students developing language skills to respond equally with others, and to get an idea of each student's understanding.

The post-Round discussion rapidly covers some of what happened. Conversation concentrates on two of Chris's Round questions—whether the groups worked productively and whether students achieved understanding—that get at the heart of the learning experience. Chris observes that one student had recently arrived from Vietnam, that his group had two students strong in English, two weak, with "no particular intellectual leader," but a "social leader." After an exchange of observations, there is general agreement that this group and others made progress in the investigation. At one point Chris's Mentor Teacher wonders aloud whether there should be some spoken acknowledgment of learning at the end of the class, some statement "of what we have learned from this experience. . . . I struggle with this after [group work]." Not having had a chance to examine the exit slips, and with the posters yet to be fully completed, members of the Round group harbor some uncertainty about what content understanding each student has developed. Chris responds hesitantly at first, "I'm not convinced there will be fragmented knowledge;" but then assumes a more confident tone and community-oriented frame of reference, "I believe we will understand." Some days later, when I again visit Chris's classroom, I see walls crowded with harmonic motion posters, each filled with illustrations, written explanations, and calculations.

Chris's Round provides a glimpse into a complex, layered, but also surpassingly focused classroom world. Chris has deep content knowledge and the ability to translate it into a powerful curriculum. He inducts students into the way of knowing of science as well, familiarizing them with the habits of mind and work practiced by scientists in the search for understanding, and giving them "the tools they need to solve complex problems they will encounter in the future." This requires an understanding of how to frame and organize content as a questioning process, as inquiry, rather than as something more objective, predigested, and inert. It also means a more complicated pedagogy, faith in a seemingly less efficient mode of learning in which puzzlement and uncertainty are affirmed, and more time than what a lockstep curriculum normally allows. Chris combines his knowledge of learners with his disciplinary and content knowledge—forming pedagogical content knowledge—to structure a process of group inquiry that builds on previous efforts, accommodates his diverse students, promotes peer collaboration, and meets his goal of equitable access and support. As they travel through the conceptual terrain, his students produce a thought trail. They document their thinking, making it visible on their exit slips and in the illustrations, equations, and explanations on their posters, giving him the feedback he needs to understand the state of their understanding.

For all this, it is also clear that Chris is developing in his understanding of scientific inquiry as a mode of classroom learning, and of group work as both a pedagogical tool and a way to make the development of knowledge a shared enterprise. He does this in part by conducting his own inquiry, with his students' learning as his subject. He is learning to measure the periodic rhythms of investigation, to measure the extent and depth of scientific inquiry his students can handle over time, to gauge a level of challenge that will be fruitful and not frustrating, and to calibrate the balance of guidance and freedom that they need at different points in their development so that all of them will reach the goal of content understanding and develop as scientific thinkers. More fundamentally, in taking their overall school experience into account in determining what his students need, and in learning how to interact with and support them, he is learning how to put belief and vision into practice in a social context. In other words, Chris is integrating content knowledge with contextual and personal knowledge in his practice. The Round process, located at the nexus and heart of the partnership community in his classroom, nurtures this evolution. It creates a small insulated space for exploring the harmonic motion of ideas and practice, for risk taking, and for a process of professional inquiry, knowledge exchange, and reflection that joins together beginning teachers like Chris and veteran teachers from the school and university.

The students in Chris's Round have the same basic destination and guiding questions. But within the framework of their teacher's careful and hopeful plan, they are provided room for personal and collective mapmaking and pathfinding, for puzzlement and uncertainty, for exploring, testing, revisiting, explaining, and staking claims. They show patience with the time and effort that it takes to question things, to explore the terrain of subject matter, to communicate their thoughts and findings—all signs, in the midst of the harmonies and disharmonies of policy, philosophy, school practice, and students' lives, of an authentic community of scientific investigators in formation.

CHAPTER 8

Chad Malone and the Muse of Authenticity

"Eyes on me."

The Claremont seventh graders fidgeting around large rectangular tables are momentarily stilled in anticipation. After 5 weeks of school they are accustomed to the authoritative and ironic tone they hear and willingly give over their easily diverted attention. No doubt they also respond to the physical presence of the teacher who looms over them—tall, rugged, athletic, dressed in jeans and a pin-striped dress shirt, scruffy, eyes defying tiredness. He is determined to engage them and make a late night of lesson planning bear fruit.

The room offers varied testimony to the learning that has taken place there during the first weeks of school. A bulletin board extending the length of one wall is crammed with pieces of chart paper, with various book and literary references. There are several scrawled messages on the blackboard. The homework assignments are in shorthand: 100 word sentence, Read OFOCNest [*One Flew Over the Cuckoo's Nest*] 260–end, d-e [double-entry journals]. The word *Transition* is barely discernible on the opposite side. These are small signs of a shared language, the beginnings of a learning community.

The hastily written notes also convey Chad's intensity of purpose and sense of urgency. When Chad exercises authority, he does so resignedly. "Eyes on me" is a concession to the need for order and collective focus. It is not the tired voice of authority seeking sycophantic submission or a truce through which teacher and students relinquish their claims on getting the best from one another. His classroom persona is in full form so as to get the rules settled and allow the real work to begin. What indeed, as he will later ask his 10th-grade students, do we learn about freedom, individuality, and institutional authority from *Cuckoo's Nest* anyway? Our time together is important. Our lives are important.

READING, WRITING, THINKING, AND LIFE

But important for what? While Chad's students will spend the year learning to be literary readers, good writers, and careful thinkers, they will also confront with him the question of the meaning of their education and their lives and how to live them. Academic capability, authenticity, and meaningfulness are intertwined educational values in Chad's philosophy, with social implications. Learning to be good readers, writers, and thinkers means acquiring powerful tools for self-discovery, learning how to live, and learning what to live for.

Chad's humanistic agenda poses challenges for his teaching. As much as the questions he wants his students to confront may seem timeless and universal, he needs to make them accessible and relevant. Can his students embrace them from their diverse perspectives and life experiences? How will he help them believe that they do not learn in order to be what others want them or try to force them to be, but in order to value and be what they are, however imperfect or flawed? How will he help them know that they have the capability and power to address and act on their answers to these questions in a world whose fairness and justice and use of power they may have very good reasons to want to change?

Chad's tools are literature, poetry, inquiry, and writing in its various forms. But he knows, in only his 3rd year of teaching, that it may take considerable time for students on the cusp of young adulthood, and to varying degrees unprepared for rigorous learning and uncertain of the meaning of school for their lives, to use these tools well. He knows the long emotional distance many students must travel before they will believe in themselves, trust in their own experience, and understand that their experience and ideas are worth sharing, and, moreover, connect them to a larger human narrative. Already he has learned to adjust to the rough terrain many students must negotiate in order to express their ideas articulately, considerately, creatively, and persuasively, to see in their efforts the possibility and value of postsecondary education, and, most of all, to see the preciousness of their own lives. Nevertheless, he feels pressure to quicken the pace, to level the playing field for his students and make school a lever of opportunity; to develop his own practice so as to safeguard minds and spirits apt otherwise to push against school as meaningless and only for kids unlike them, and slip away. The question that lies in wait every school night is "how."

The policy environment offers little to encourage Chad. As much as self-understanding and authentic learning—learning that connects to real experience—might strike an intuitive chord as educational values and suggest a powerful way of being in the classroom, they are not well-represented in reform. Set against the hard-edged rhetoric of economic competitiveness and the emphasis on quantifying academic proficiency, they appear as soft, nonutilitarian, and inexpedient. At best they are caught in the tension between measurability and meaningfulness that underlies reform and that is expressed in curriculum development. Chad, on the one hand, can draw on the state English language arts curriculum framework for support (Massachusetts Department of Elementary and Secondary Education, 2001). As one of its guiding principles, for instance, the framework highlights the importance of cultivating the distinctive writing or speaking voice of each student as "an expression of self," enabling students to tell us who they are, what they think, and what unique perspectives they bring to their learning and to each other (p. 6). Nearer to home, however, the policies hew closely to a common program for test readiness and appear more constraining. The district recently launched an effort to synchronize the curriculum so that teachers at the same grade level are using the same texts more or less at the same time.

Tensions in curricular philosophy at different levels of the educational system—between, for example, a teacher's philosophical position and systemwide curricular plans—are not unusual. Partly, they reflect different responses to accountability measures and the pressure for results; partly, a judgment on where curricular decision making best lies, whether at a macro- or a microlevel, whether in the hands of policy makers, district leaders, school leaders, communities, or teachers. Often they result from a simplified idea, on the policy side, of the everyday tasks of teachers. Chad, for his part, appreciates the broad principles of the framework and values district curricular examples on their own merits. Like most teachers, however, he also values and needs room for independent judgment and creativity when it comes to curriculum and how to implement it so as to best serve his particular students at a given moment of time. Take away this judgment, and he and his students must struggle to follow an external plan disconnected from themselves and the unique learning process that forms when students, subject matter, and teacher interact in a particular place and time.

VOCATIONAL VERSUS INSTITUTIONAL COMMUNITIES

The question of students brings us back to the classroom scene and the beginning of a Round. Thirteen students sit before Chad: 6 girls and 7 boys; several are absent. Shades of black and brown predominate in the human color scheme of the room, with Chad's wavy red hair standing starkly alone at one end of the spectrum. The color contrast, together with the poverty of many of his students, underscore the social import of his task. Five students in the Master of Arts in Teaching program cluster in the back of the room with their professor, completing the group.

Chad asks the MATs to introduce themselves and tells the class that "when I have my friends here I want them to help." The Round for Chad is not an exhibition, not, as he says, a "game day." It is instead a chance to talk about real practice, and to enhance the learning experience. It also personifies and familiarizes his Claremont students with the university culture; this acculturation process is embedded in UPCS and helps make the university seem accessible, especially to students whose families have no college-going experience. Chad is also sensitive to what might benefit the MATs. He is acutely aware of the questions, concerns, doubts, and hopes that dominate their young teaching lives at the moment.

The Round reminds Chad of the collegial atmosphere he enjoyed in the MAT program, both with his peers and at UPCS. Imbued with UPCS conviction and culture following his year there as an MAT, Chad felt a strong contrast upon his arrival at Claremont. At UPCS a vivid and unifying sense of mission and continuous learning-centered and student-focused discussion dominate the cultural discourse, but Claremont was laboring to meet the challenge of reculturing in the wake of state scrutiny and its reconfiguration as a Grades 7–12 school. The school had been set on its heels; hope and commitment were guarded, mixing uneasily with routine compliance, cautiousness, and defensiveness. Chad did not walk into the corridor from his classroom and participate in the customary and reflective exchange about curriculum, practice, and kids that occurs as a matter of course at UPCS. The Round group thus provides a moment's infusion of the professional oxygen that, like most teachers, he needs and craves.

What Chad noticed missing at Claremont was the sustaining presence of a sense of common purpose, moral and intellectual commitment, and practice. At UPCS he experienced a vocational community, one with a strong sense of calling. The school's mission, beliefs, relationships, structure, practice, and culture cohered with moral resolve. He had a taste of what it might mean to bring himself wholly to the work of awakening kids' minds, with the fortifying knowledge that his colleagues were supporting each other in the effort. This is not at all to say that a sense of vocation did not exist among his colleagues at Claremont when he arrived. But in terms of its cultural life Claremont was functioning more as an institutional entity than a vocational community. Its culture was shaped more by heavy external demands than by internal conviction, its vocational sensibilities to some extent benumbed by the intensified pressure of accountability.

The institutional expectations and mandates leading up to and including its designation as a state "underperforming" school more than a year before Chad's coming, and before its restructuring as Claremont Academy, had narrowed the sense of mission, cultural discourse, practice, and community at the school. Although in its fact-finding report the Massachusetts

Department of Elementary and Secondary Education (2005) endeavored to identify "the enabling elements that make instructional improvement possible," this translated at the school level to dogmatic attention to state standards, deficits in performance, state test scores, and changing the school's underperformance status (p. 1). Teachers put curriculum objectives on their whiteboards to show adherence to "standards-based teaching." In rare moments, as time allowed, they looked at data to identify student strengths and target weaknesses in mathematics and English language arts. But, as Chad had come to know, there can be a long pedagogical path between the idea of a standard or some determination of student needs and actual student understanding. Likewise, he knew that standards and data, divorced from larger beliefs, values, purposes, and principles of practice, can inadvertently diminish the possibilities for engagement and authentic learning. There was little in the way of a unifying force in this mandated approach, little of the vocational or spiritual adhesive necessary for forming a powerful learning community for adults as well as the students entering his classes. Its absence for someone like Chad was palpable.

Against this backdrop of policy, institutional history, and school culture, Chad is intent on engaging his young students with the conviction that their lives—and his—depend on it. This is not at all to say that he casts himself as a savior or that he lacks humility. But he has an acute awareness of what is at stake for his students and what is possible for them as learners. Teaching in a certain sense is his Walden Pond. Like Henry David Thoreau (1854/1996) meditating at Walden, Chad "did not wish to live what was not life," but rather "to live deep" (p. 82). Just as Thoreau wanted to "live deliberately," he gives himself deliberately to the task. He also has to guard against personal doubt, tune out cultural dissonance, and avoid a vain and ultimately self-defeating effort to force results. He has to trust himself, overcome the fear of taking risks in isolation. At UPCS, and with the support of his university mentors as a graduate student, he felt protected from being so exposed.

ENGAGING ALL STUDENTS IN READING, WRITING, SPEAKING, AND THINKING

Today is one of many necessary small steps in moving his students forward. The seventh graders are preparing to put a character from a short story titled "Confession" on trial. Chad flips on the overhead projector, illuminating a sheet listing the roles in the trial (police, defense lawyers, prosecuting lawyers, judges), and then, literally on his knees as if in earnest supplication, hand slamming a nearby desk for emphasis, instructs, "To prosecute someone is to find them guilty. . . . Make an argument . . . why they should be found guilty—send these hooligans off to jail! You need at least six reasons from the story." As an aside to members of the Round group he acknowledges, "I want to get good at trials . . . next week [the initial efforts] will be a mess." But Chad understands that messiness may be a necessary stage in learning.

The students are just learning the mechanics and argumentative moves of a trial. The trial itself is a device to get them digging into text: pulling it apart, debating its meaning, using it to construct arguments. The text is not long, and before they are through with trial preparation the students will know it thoroughly. Chad's handout with guided reading questions helps. The questions are designed to stimulate basic comprehension and take nothing for granted; one, for example, asks, "What happens at the end of the story?" Students also keep journals to respond to the text; if they have not already, they will soon realize that reading, writing, and informal and formal speaking are inextricably intertwined elements of learning in this class.

The content has some resonance for them, as the "hooligans" in the story are kids, and the seventh graders undertake scrutiny of their actions willingly. The setting and tone are urban, gritty. There is gang activity and good intentions to curb it—but they cannot forestall violence. Things go wrong when they are not supposed to; and, in putting the protagonist on trial, students must grapple with the question of legal and moral responsibility for unintended consequences.

Students work sporadically in groups or in pairs, clutching blue notebook journals with recorded thoughts about the text, Chad checking on them. A few prepare summaries based on their roles in the trial on chart paper. One girl, warming up to the role of chief prosecutor, her red, heart-shaped earrings glittering confidently, listens to several students' interpretations of the text, debating at one point whether having a gun is preparing for self-defense or a sign of intent. Her disputant, pausing as if surprised to hear herself say the word, insists, "It's injustice! . . . on page 110 . . . he was provoking him! It's all seriously messed up!" This is a positive exclamation of frustration and confusion, a student engaged enough to care about what she does not yet understand. One or two other moments of passionate and anxious exchange punctuate the conversations; otherwise there are hurried efforts to get thoughts onto chart paper. Though more intent perhaps on completing given assignments than on developing and disciplining their arguments, and very much novices in the art of collaboration, these seventh-grade students are working with a fair degree of independence and absorption at this early stage of the year. They are becoming unwitting accomplices in Chad's pedagogy: That is to say, they are beginning to read, write, think, and act on their own. The class ends with students still scurrying to complete their trial preparation, Chad musing that they might have "a trial run for the trial."

There is no time for a post-Round conversation, so we do not learn any more about Chad's assessment of his students' progress. Instead, Chad greets his 11th-grade class as they meander in, a study in affected adolescent nonchalance. As they settle, he tells the Round group that this class is "underinformed" about current events and basic research skills. So he has formed them into "expert teams" of four, each team responsible for a sizzling conversation on a hot topic of their own choice (choice is presumably motivating, although topics must be approved by Chad), using a "Socratic seminar" format and protocol.

Today's group will discuss the ongoing war in Iraq. The four team members face each other, chairs in a tight circle. Their peers form a circle around them, with Round participants interspersed. Each member of the group of four is allowed no more than two index cards with reference material. Members of the outer circle may only take notes. Chad tasks the members of the outer circle with discerning who in the inner circle has "read the text closely, citing textual evidence and examples in the discussion," and who has "to rely on B.S. to get through the discussion." Each member of the outer circle has a specific observation task as well, such as identifying "the most outrageous thing you hear," "the point you agree with most," or "an insightful comment"; they will present their observation data after the 15-minute discussion period. They are to be perceptive listeners and critical friends, charged with being fair and honest without being grating or raw. All will write 1–2 page reaction papers; their counterparts in the inner circle will assess in writing the credibility of one of the articles they have read in preparing for their seminar discussion. The reaction papers should raise more questions than answers. Chad wants his students to refrain from a knee-jerk and expedient tendency toward simplification and reductionism in their thinking and to uncover the complexity of serious topics. He is pushing them hard to cultivate a habit of thoughtful examination and critical inquiry.

One of the students in the expert team acts as facilitator and announces the objectives of the discussion, such as identifying reasons for the war. Though remarkably perceptive, his questioning of his three peers is relentless—more prosecutorial than facilitative—and ends up stifling the flow of discussion within the group. Arguments about the reasons for the war, its consequences, and alternative courses of action beg for sharper definition, although the discussion shows signs of substantial investigation. Yet at its conclusion Chad says, "You guys tap-danced for 15 minutes." Constructive criticisms waft inward from the outer circle. "[They] said we went for oil, but didn't give any facts—evidence—to back it up. . . . We're in Iraq: what do we do?"

What has transpired? Students in the class as a whole have pondered the political, economic, and moral questions that surround the war, significant in itself. Yet it is unclear who in the inner circle is ready to articulate and substantiate a particular stand. The lesson learned is that facile opinions will not gain much traction in this class, that researched and well-reasoned arguments will have a much longer and more fruitful lifespan. Habits of mind, therefore, are being honed, and culturally the class has moved a step closer to adopting fundamental norms of argumentation and scholarship. However awkwardly, students have entered an early stage in their formation as a community of young scholars.

Though it may not be as readily apparent, the Round group also witnesses Chad's determined effort to turn personal conviction into powerful learning for his students. The trial role-play and the Socratic seminar are "best practice" learning strategies in the sense that they engage all students productively in the fundamental activities of reading, writing, speaking, and thinking. But they must be well-timed and constructed in terms of students' academic development in order to be beneficial. Chad has to model them and guide students into them, and he is still refining this process; both classes, for instance, will need more practice in sorting evidence and building arguments. But even more, he has to help students believe in the value of the learning process and in themselves as learners. It is one thing to design activities to build academic capability and lead students to confident participation in the academic world, quite another to make these activities meaningful. It is not enough for students to engage out of trust in him and his purposes, although that will serve well enough as a starting point; they must trust in themselves and the efficacy of their effort.

It is impossible for students to believe in themselves and the value of school and to invest themselves, if they do not sense their teacher's belief in them and if they do not feel a connection to their personal lives and hidden hopes. They enter the world of formal meaning represented by school more willingly if they perceive its meaning for themselves and a possible place in it for themselves, if, especially as they get older, they can make the link between their present and future lives. Mastery of the academic world may be their passport into advanced learning and an educated workforce, but what will motivate them to want to qualify, in particular if their lives are unstable and uncertain? And what will convince them that each has one precious life, that school will help build their capacity and freedom to choose it, and that society will make a place for them? They may not need reason to hope, as hope, noted by Chad in class, evoking Emily Dickinson (n.d.), is "the thing with feathers that perches in the soul" (p. 34). But what reason do they have to strive and aspire in school, to give hope wings?

HARNESSING THE POWER OF LANGUAGE AND WRITING

Chad cannot be true to himself and what he perceives as the teaching vocation without taking into consideration these educational questions and social and existential concerns. As briefly glimpsed in the Round classes, his effort to empower students with academic capability and at the same time help them discover meaning and possibility in their own lives combines real-life issues with academic and intellectual work. But there is one theme that is not fully represented in the Rounds. Chad wants students to learn to write. Writing is his principal means for helping them develop their ideas, their voices, and connections between their personal and academic worlds; for harnessing their hopes and sense of self to aspiration and new possibility.

As scholars have pointed out and illustrated, language is culturally situated.[1] School cultures specialize in academic discourse—a code of learning dense with its own purposes, forms, and meanings. The academic code is as foreign as any language for students who enter it from home lives in which the normal daily ways of communicating and relating are much different. Indeed, whereas many students, most from middle-class families with college-educated parents, have practice with the modes of learning and communication in schools, others will encounter them as if a foreign and forbidding land. If students fail to master them, they lack the wherewithal to participate in the academic culture of shared knowledge and discourse. They lack the social capital and negotiating capability typically used to leverage entry into higher education and our knowledge-based economy, and therefore the ability to secure their best opportunities as well. Echoing Jim McDermott, one of his mentors at the Hiatt Center, Chad says they lack "the language of the powerful." Learning to write will be their rite of passage into a broader, educated world.

Chad's program for developing his students as writers is inspired by McDermott. Jim exhorts Hiatt Center graduate students and teachers to "empower kids to do great stuff," and, in spite of a compelling record in this regard, challenges no one more than he does himself to demonstrate how. He is unabashed in his conviction that kids learning to write well and writing that links to "the soul" go hand in hand. His passion for teaching is effusive and infectious. Chad's continuing connection to Jim and the Hiatt Center helps sustain his effort.

Chad's writing curriculum begins with the humble sentence. The sentence is a fundamental building block in good writing and, in Chad's view, "the basic unit of thought." But writing good ones, even the simple declarative ones, can be a demanding task for many students. Its humble role does not make the sentence any less complex nor, on the face of it, any more interesting. Good written sentences do not conform readily to casual street talk, although, particularly in narrative-descriptive writing, they might share some of the same sense and rhythm; nor do sentences grow easily from the rapid, sound-bite repartee of television. While students may encounter them in good literature, the mysteries of their construction, and sometimes their meaning, often confound them. Chad must overcome students' wariness of the sentence, on the one hand, and learned distaste for the austerities of grammar, on the other, all the while making the idea of writing a sentence an inviting if not deliciously appealing activity. He must, in other words, translate the idea of mastering the written sentence into classroom practice.

In developing his practice, Chad trusts in the fundamental creative power of language. Students already have some understanding of the power of words in their everyday use of language. They may enjoy inventing words and word combinations and playing with the sounds and meanings. They may appreciate the way language can be adapted and molded to make unique expressions or expressions with unique social meaning in a family, a group of friends, a neighborhood, or some other setting. Chad wants to introduce students to the sentence without sacrificing the existentially satisfying qualities and playfulness of language. He wants them to enter the demanding discipline of formal writing with a sense of capacity and meaningfulness. There is an echo of Robert Frost's theory of poetry in this orientation. His students could easily do worse than begin to write from a sense of delight, and reach some small clarification of life and modest enhancement of their sense of being in the process, thereby constructing a "momentary stay against confusion," or against uncertainty (Perkins, 1972, p. 209).

Visiting Chad's classroom one day early in the fall, I see projected onto the whiteboard what looks to be a long passage from a book, and I expect to hear some kind of literary discussion. Chad reads the text with just enough awe to evoke a respectful silence in the room. It is indeed a fair piece of writing, but its source is one of the students in the class. And what appeared to be a passage is in fact a single sentence, albeit one which cascades relentlessly down the page, leaving behind an impressive spray of interconnected verb and noun clusters. Here is about half, comprising over 90 words:

> As I laid on my bed, staring, I could see everything about my mom, her fat jiggling, her long half-grayed hair, her thick round glasses, her fake dentures, her dull black pants, her worn out old style jacket wrapped around her, the way she slowly walks toward the kitchen, the way her skin wrinkles up, her gigantic thighs swaying back and forth, her crusty fingers holding onto a bowl, her feet resting on the chair beside her, her eyes squinting tightly, her running nose, her face attached with a frown that will forever stay. . . .

The piece raises questions about rhythm and repetition, but for now the length and effort at vivid language gain the most attention. I might have recognized the form at first glance, as I had seen such sentences before in Jim McDermott's room during his teaching days as an English teacher at UPCS. The reading concludes with a ritual count of the number of words. As it turns out, Chad's students are writing *cumulative sentences*. The word count is partly motivational play, partly a measure of their progress toward mastering the structure of a powerful sentence. Their goal, approached in tantalizing increments, is at least 100 words.

Later in the fall Chad explains his strategic use of the cumulative sentence during a presentation at the Hiatt Center's First Annual Partnership Best Practice Workshop. The room is crowded with teachers and Master of Arts in Teaching students, the district superintendent of schools sitting among them. This is Chad's most public presentation as a teacher and forces him to articulate his practice. Keeping a brisk pace, trying to compress several months of valued work in a 45-minute time frame, he alternates between commenting on his students' work and engaging members of the audience in constructing their own cumulative sentences. To establish his philosophical position, he intersperses references to *Notes Toward a New Rhetoric: Nine Essays for Teachers* (Christensen & Christensen, 1978), citing it with biblical fervor.

Christensen and Christensen explain that the cumulative sentence contains a main clause together with modifiers that add to, amplify, extend, and texture its meaning. They note that it appears regularly in the prose of writers, such as Faulkner and Ellison, who practice the craft at its highest level. A position embraced by teachers like Chad and Jim McDermott, Christensen and Christensen insist that "we should teach our students to write the way we see practiced craftsmen write" (p. 22). They are not preaching simple imitation, however, but the virtues of "cumulative." In constructing a cumulative sentence, one constructs its meaning as well, as each potential modifier needs disciplined consideration of the meaning it adds to the main clause. Christensen and Christensen elaborate:

> The typical sentence of modern English, the kind we can best spend our efforts trying to teach, is what we may call the *cumulative sentence*. The main clause, which may or may not have a sentence modifier before it, advances the discussion; but the additions move backward, as in this clause, to modify the statement of the main clause or more often to explicate or exemplify it, so that the sentence has a flowing and ebbing movement, advancing to a new position and then pausing to consolidate it, leaping and lingering as the popular ballad does. . . . The cumulative sentence . . . is dynamic rather than static, representing the mind thinking. (pp. 27–28)

Chad's pedagogical thinking adheres fast to the latter point: the thinking that is nurtured by the process of constructing it, that the actual writing makes visible, gives the cumulative sentence its personal and pedagogical as well as rhetorical value. Chad calls cumulative sentences "thinking sentences." In an astute teacher's hands they become a window into students' thoughts as well as their understanding of what makes a sentence powerful.

They also become life affirming. In fulfilling their purpose to illuminate a main idea, cumulative sentences demand a faithful rendering of what is real. In their discussion of narrative-descriptive writing, Christensen and Christensen emphasize that sentence modifiers should be based on personal observation. Students therefore need practice in observing, noticing, and giving attention to what is before them; if they begin to pay attention, they "begin to look at life with more alertness" (p. 38). Every student has sensory impressions to bring to the task, which makes it accessible; each is challenged to turn impressions into clear prose, which makes the task conducive to careful diction. The cumulative sentence can become a powerful vehicle for developing and communicating student awareness of the world around them: "This can hardly fail to be exciting to a class: it is life, with the variety and complexity of life; the workbook exercise is death" (p. 35).

To keep the focus on thoughtful formulation, the process of writing cumulative sentences is grammar-free. Once students gain confidence in producing them, grammatical analysis, otherwise counterproductive and devoid of life, makes some sense; "from then on the grammar comes to the aid of the writing and the writing reinforces the grammar" (Christensen and Christensen, p. 35). Students who have learned to flex their verbal muscles through the construction of cumulative sentences also more readily parse other texts. According to Christensen and Christensen, there are innumerable examples of cumulative sentences in the literature students are expected to read, and the ability to penetrate these syntactical mysteries, and to appreciate their meaning, is immeasurably improved if they have successfully produced a dazzling example or two themselves.

In Chad's pedagogical rendering of the cumulative sentence, play and practice combine much as they do on the basketball court. As coach of the girls' team and a former player himself, Chad knows that success comes from the right balance of creativity, strategic play, and discipline. He gives students ample opportunity to explore the possibilities of clauses and phrases and how they clarify or amplify meaning, to play with words and structure, and to make their sentences impressive, not simply long. "Writing is messy, not neat," Chad explains. "Let it be messy and confusing." His understanding of the value of "messing around" with language for the development of his diverse students' understanding of its possibilities is a critical component of his pedagogy. One of his strategies is to ask students to configure as many sentences as they can from the separate phrases and clauses he gives them on index cards. Chad's students will work their way into written formalities, demystifying them, exploring their many contours, getting comfortable with them, manipulating them, making them more and more their own. At the same time, they will practice to the point of "brutal repetition," and Chad has to remind them that he wants to see "precise, telling detail."

Consider one student, writing in response to Salinger's *Catcher in the Rye*: "I agree with Holden. Life is a bitch, but I'm still blowing kisses at it." Chad remarks in his presentation at the Best Practice Workshop that the sentence has pithiness, with some raw power, but is limited in what it conveys. It reflects a writer trying on a persona, playing with tone. The tone suggests the defiance and cavalier resentment that Chad finds smoldering beneath the demeanor of some of his students, which often mask deeper emotions, such as fear that there is no real place for them in the world.

Chad encourages more concrete detail, and for that student, Holden eventually exchanges blown kisses for revealing particulars and pathos:

> Holden remembers everything about Allie and his baseball mitt, the green writing, the poems scratched into the glove, how Allie would read it when he was standing in the outfield, waiting for the game, and the way his life was taken by leukemia like a burglar in the night.

Thus Chad turns a sparse, underdeveloped sentence into an opportunity to cultivate attentiveness to detail and human experience. He asks this student to develop awareness, show understanding, and to write with care, not to fulfill an empty academic purpose or to prepare for a test. As Christensen and Christensen suggest, learning to attend so as to write powerfully, and writing so as to learn to attend, taps into students' thirst for understanding themselves and life in general; it invites honest exploration of inner as well as outer worlds. Writing in this sense, to borrow again from observer-naturalist Thoreau (1996), is helping students learn to live awake.

In the spirit of play, students learn to enjoy language; through practice, they learn to bring disciplined attention and authenticity as well as creativity to writing. This approach is intentionally low risk and low stakes; the idea is to reconnect with language on a basic level, to get a feel for its power and confidence in handling it. And students learn a great deal about sentence construction in the process. In due course they will be able to point out the noun phrase, verb clusters, adjective clusters, prepositional phrases containing similes, and the "mandatory moves" or rhetorical features of their verbal constructions, just as Chad's basketball players can name the crossover dribble, the bounce pass, the slide-step, and the box-out, and what they mean to the game as a whole. The 100-word threshold draws them forward like a championship quest, and each shared sentence builds communal appreciation.

Having worked extensively on the cumulative sentence, Chad's students will revisit the paragraph and the elements that make one powerful. But his writing program is not a simple sequence from one element of composition to another. Even as they explore, create, practice, and examine writing within the parameters of each essential element, students will write extensively, responding to literature in journals, responding to writing prompts, composing short reaction papers and essays. Their study and practice of writing combine with opportunities to write on matters of personal and literary import. Chad aims through this process to cultivate their own voices—"no voice, no power," as he puts it.

As much as it is vital, voice can be frustratingly elusive. How do experience and perspective find words, and how do words come together in a distinctive pattern? How does one attain an authentic expression of self? How does voice change from genre to genre—how is the writer present in informal writing as compared to formal, in narrative as compared to persuasive or expository forms? And where and for what reason is there courage to travel across the boundary between personal and public? If words and ideas exist like inseparable and attentive partners in a dance, with writing the music that moves them, then the teacher's job is to help students listen to the music and trust in the dance. So often when I enter Chad's classroom, I enter a small world of silence, students and Chad both with heads down, pens poised or in motion, faces absorbed or abstracted or wearing their uncertainty.

AWAKENING INNER LIVES AND MINDS

Students need help attending to inner experience and the muse of authenticity—in using writing as a way to draw out and clarify what is real in themselves—even as they apprentice to writing's various forms. The classroom therefore must serve at times as a kind of sanctuary, a place where inner lives and intellectual discipline can safely awaken and mature; where, to recall the example above, Holden, in the mind and heart of a student, can acquire compassion. To view school as a sacred space is not typical; but it is in keeping with teaching's moral purpose to see it so. The development of voice is an act of faith in and respect for the value of each student, a recognition of their lives as precious; the awakening of their inner lives becomes an affirmation of each of us, of the life and hopes we share.

Thomas Merton (1979) writes that "every act, however small, can teach you everything—provided you see who it is that is acting" (p. 14). To the extent that we understand every teaching action as a mirror of ourselves, and have courage equal to what we want to see there, we begin to honor the preciousness of the lives of our students as well as our own. We not only in this sense teach what we are, but also what we believe: about our students and their possible futures, about knowledge and what is worth knowing, about how young people learn and what they need. For Chad, the cumulative sentence is a means not an end. It is meant first of all to help educate the capacity for inner awareness and attentive thought and facility in voicing it. Second, it is part of the academic understanding necessary for leveraging greater opportunity in a complex social world. Thus it serves as a tool for both self-discovery and social efficacy. It reflects the moral as well as spiritual, or life-affirming, purposes that pulse through Chad's developing practice, and also its social and political edge.

In the eyes of education reform, the practice of teaching is commonly viewed as delivering subject matter in conformity to curricular principles and high standards, with corresponding high expectations. Many would add the use of research-based methods of learning to this definition. But the persistent gaps in achievement based on income level or minority status beg for a more complex perspective. As helpful as principles, standards and methods can be, practice is more than their sum. When it comes to developing a coherent and powerful practice—one that embraces diverse students and fosters academic capability in the interest of authenticity, social efficacy, and a level playing field of opportunity—a teacher's integrity and vocational commitment (sense of moral purpose, beliefs, and educational values), disciplinary knowledge, and strategic judgment aimed at building students' trust, self-belief, acceptance of challenge, and aspiration also matter.

Chad's effort to align moral, spiritual, and social purposes and weave them together with disciplinary understanding and knowledge of learning, curricular goals, and policy, as well as contextual knowledge of students and their lives into a teaching practice is complicated. Like the development of good writing, the development of a coherent and powerful practice can be messy, confusing, and tenuous. Personal and cultural support— through, for example, Rounds and other forms of collaborative learning that build shared understandings and values—provide much more room for the strategic play, attentive discipline, and enormous reflective effort involved.

Good practice requires a trusting and believing relationship with students, a relationship that allows for informed judgments. It needs, as well, a culture in which challenges can be met with mutual support. Facing a blowout during the first half of one of their games, Chad in a soft but firm voice points out to members of the girls' basketball team during a timeout that this is an example of adversity, and an opportunity to face up to it. They tighten the defense, begin to move the ball more effectively, and make the game respectable.

CHAPTER 9

Making More from Less: Ways of Knowing History

GATHERED AROUND A table in the Claremont Academy library, nine students try to make sense of a black and white nineteenth century family photograph. On the grainy left side of the photograph, a mother holds a small child in her lap. Two other small children, expressions rather glum, are seated in front of her, each with dresses, although one appears to be a boy. To the right a young boy stands next to a seated man, presumably his father. Another man sits to the rear of them with arms folded. No one is smiling. The adults are seated on either side of a table decorated with flowers and a white fringed tablecloth, and laden with several books of biblical heft. Most intriguing of all, they are all outside, with a trim picket fence and a clapboard house composing the background of the strange and solemn domestic scene.

Amy Richter, the instructor, asks what strikes them about the picture. Students respond that "they brought their kitchen stuff outside" and want to "show off their house." Amy builds on these observations—"they also need to show off the inside . . . those things that will identify them as moral"— and confirms that it was necessary to set the scene outside the house because of poor lighting. She emphasizes that the photograph is meant to convey a particular message; though located outside because of photographic necessity, it displays enough of the interior decor to demonstrate the moral uprightness of the family's domestic life. She thus transforms an old family portrait into a historical artifact and suggests how curiosity can turn into historical investigation.

The students examine several other photographs. One comes from a sales catalog of the late nineteenth century and depicts a set of parlor chairs. A student mentions that the chairs do not look comfortable. Amy asks whether it looks "like something you can slouch on." She then comments that the parlor was "a kind of public space" in your home and that the straight backs of the chairs reflect a belief that the physical and the moral reinforce one another. People sat upright in those chairs and looked one another in the eye as an expression of moral rectitude.

Amy is a historian at Clark University with a special interest in U.S. women's history. She offered to facilitate a weekly seminar for high school students during the spring term on the meaning of home "then and now," and the students—10th and 11th graders from UPCS and Claremont, both boys and girls—volunteered to give it a try. Amy's seminar is one of several running at the schools this year; the others, addressing urban ecology, Shakespeare, literature, and social authority and moral perception, are facilitated by professors of geography, theater, English, and sociology, respectively. The seminars serve an important role in the school partnerships. University faculty members, usually with help from a colleague from the Hiatt Center, design them to introduce students to new intellectual worlds and, more generally, to the tools of investigation and ways of thinking used by scholars. Part of their purpose is to demystify academic knowledge, to show its personal face and dynamic qualities; and part is to familiarize students with college, show that it is accessible, and build their aspiration and resolve to qualify for admission.

Summarizing the examination of the photographs, Amy makes sure to accentuate the central role of curiosity and inquiry in her work as a historian, and its real-life focus. The people in the photographs "have a whole system of values . . . this is what it means to make sense of the past—what is fun for me is to figure them out, to understand them. . . . Historians try to understand people by studying their stuff." She also introduces them to the idea that historians define and try to solve problems, which often means working through disagreements in interpretation. As she puts it, "The other thing I carry around in my head" is what historians interested in women and who study the home ("that's where women were") think about women's status and power. That comment segues to the students' next task: to read two poems about a woman's role in the home and decide whether they reflect the same view of status and power.

MAKING SENSE OF THE PAST

Making sense of the past is not simple for students. One reason is that history is not necessarily represented in curriculum in the way that a historian such as Amy lives with it—as a matter of curiosity, investigation, problem solving, and coconstructed interpretation, as a response to the innate and insistent desire to understand the connection between then and now, between who "we" in the past were and who "we" in the present are. Historians explore and document the human story. They are detectives of the past, striving to determine what happened and its significance for us. They learn to exercise discriminating hindsight and to judiciously compile evidence of what people thought and did, and why. By comparison and contrast they try to help us understand our own ways of being and acting in the world, and the potential consequences for the future. Their findings influence our understanding of the human experience, more particularly our collective sense of identity and direction.

Yet students rarely encounter this dynamic quality and relevance of historical study, if at all; neither do they come to understand the often painstaking and lengthy steps that historians must take in their quest to uncover the past. Instead they regard the past as inert and static, as a dense and relentless parade of disconnected and immutable facts. Curricula variously counter or aid and abet this perception. The current Massachusetts curriculum framework, for example, is a compendium of topics covering large swaths of the vast field of history (Massachusetts Department of Elementary and Secondary Curriculum, 2003). Coverage instead of inquiry becomes the operative word. Teachers feel pressure to march through the curriculum, and the forced march leaves students with a dim sense of the past and its vitality vis-à-vis the present. History becomes "boring."

Understanding the past may involve more subtle issues as well. In *Historical Thinking and Other Unnatural Acts: Charting the Future of Teaching the Past* (2001) Sam Wineburg uncovers some of the cognitive challenges involved in making sense of the past. For one thing, we must try to account for our natural reliance on our present-day understandings as a lens for interpreting history. As Wineburg's research shows, for example, one student might conclude that Lincoln was a racist, another take a more cautious stance upon reading Lincoln's reply to Stephen A. Douglas of August 21, 1858: "I agree with Judge Douglas [that the Negro] is not my equal in many respects—certainly not in color, perhaps not in moral or intellectual endowment" (p. 97). The difference lies in whether a student goes beyond simply reading and judging the words in relation to her or his current view of racism and tries to situate and understand them in their context, in relation to the mind-set and circumstances under which they were spoken. We would see evidence of such contextualizing when students begin to question, as historians do, why Lincoln said what he did. Wineburg found that students (college level in his study) do not contextualize and empathize automatically. Even when confronted with texts that illuminate the prevailing views about race that Lincoln would assume in his audience and show nuance in his thinking, a student might resist qualifying or changing the perception of racism. To nurture historical thinking, students need evidence that confronts their taken-for-granted preconceptions—the kind of cognitive nudging that Amy was instigating in giving students photographs that challenged them to see beyond what they consider natural family behavior.

In fact, one of the students in Wineburg's research was a history major preparing to teach. His historical thinking happened to be much less contextually sensitive than that demonstrated by the historians Wineburg consulted to provide a measure of comparison. As Wineburg suggests, this student's tendency to impose the present on the past, his limited depth perception, raises the question of how we construe what is adequate as content knowledge in teacher preparation. Policy that equates subject matter preparation with the number of content courses a student has taken may be as flawed as curriculum that treats historical knowledge as a comprehensive collection of topics. In determining "teacher quality" and subject matter expertise, much depends on whether we want K–12 students to progress in the kind of thinking that Amy does, on how we want them to "know" history.

DEVELOPING HISTORICAL MINDS AND KNOWLEDGE WITH RICCI HALL

Ricci Hall, a graduate student at UPCS when the school opened, and now the only active teacher who dates his tenure at the school from its beginning, strives to balance depth with breadth in the curriculum in order to foster both historical thinking and knowledge. One of the tools he and other history teachers at UPCS use with their students, developed by the Hiatt Center History Curriculum Team, of which Ricci has been a member, is called *Primary Source Circles*. These extend the literature circle idea into the history classroom in much the same way that Jody Bird (see Chapter 6) incorporates it into her science classes. It is a collaborative learning strategy that incorporates individual roles matched to basic attributes of historical thinking and investigation.

The student roles for Primary Source Circles align in particular with the historian's effort to understand point of view and historical context; establish reliable and helpful historical evidence; question, interpret, and speculate; and compare historical and current perspectives. For example, a student in the role of *Author* looks for information that might explain the point of view of the author of a particular document. The student representing *Audience* establishes who might have been the author's intended or expected listeners or readers and how that audience might have influenced the text or artifact. The focus of the *Time Researcher* is to build historical context—to bring information from the time period and the specific social, political, or cultural context that might be relevant for understanding the source. Each of these roles has several tasks assigned to it. The tasks are placed in a general order of sophistication; thus students progress from simple to more complex levels of investigation, progressing according to their experience and capabilities at a given point in time. As an example, the tasks for a student playing the role of Author begin with finding information about the author and progress to reflecting on how her or his own beliefs might influence thinking about the author.

Students practice each role under teacher guidance as they learn how to examine primary source documents and "do" history. After sufficient practice they perform and rotate the roles in small groups. Sometimes, if all the groups in a class are analyzing the same source, students who are performing the same roles come together to compare and develop their notes. This learning process takes time and, depending on the students' academic development, can easily last a whole year or more.

Primary Source Circles are one way to scaffold thinking central to the way historians come to know history, to cultivate the habits of mind that might appear, in Wineburg's apt term, "unnatural" to students. Benefiting from a curriculum that has done this from their 1st year in the school, Ricci's 11th-grade students have internalized Primary Source Circles to the point where he does not use them formally. Nevertheless, he is careful to raise questions that ask for good historical thinking as a matter of course, challenging students to discuss the credibility of a source or to put it in the context of its time. In this way he strives to deepen students' understanding of major events of U.S. history, as he indicates in the background section of his Round sheet for today's class.

At the same time, he asks them to discern connections and differences in relation to the present day, to tease out the influential continuities and contingencies of history; this is one aspect of his effort to cultivate what he calls a "historical mind." One of his Round questions reflects this emphasis: "To what extent did students put the arguments [in the texts by W. E. B. Dubois and Booker T. Washington that they are reading] in the historical context of the times, in order to locate their rationale? Make connections between the periods before and after these arguments, including the present?" Ricci is asking Round participants to listen for evidence of good historical thinking in the class.

The 11th graders in Ricci's group are self-selected members of his Advanced Placement class in American history. Advanced Placement classes at UPCS are open enrollment—any student is eligible to take them. To encourage student participation, the AP classes are not offered separately from other classes, but rather as a supplement to them. All classes at UPCS run 4 days a week. Wednesday is an alternative flexible day, allowing students to participate in seminars such as Amy's and to take supplementary subject matter classes based on need or interest or, as in this case, for AP credit. The 12 students in Ricci's group represent close to a third of the entire junior class. They take their regular American history class 4 days a week, which, like all high school classes at UPCS, is taught at an honors level. They meet with Ricci for an AP session every Wednesday, thereby extending the learning in their regular class. In between weekly classes Ricci asks them to develop note cards on the basic "who" and "what" of the history they are studying, which he checks. During class time on Wednesdays they conduct in-depth primary source analysis and develop historical thinking.

The purpose of today's class is to compare, contrast, and put into historical perspective "The Talented Tenth" by W. E. B. Dubois and Booker T. Washington's "Atlanta Exposition Address, 1893." Ricci summarizes his purpose on his Round sheet:

> Ultimately I want students to think critically about the complicated theories presented by both figures. Additionally, I want students to appreciate the time period in which these theories were presented and the ways that we have come to understand them since. I want them also to confront how the bias of our twenty-first-century eyes can impact the way we view the thinking of people of the past.

Students enter the class having read one of the documents, and having prepared notes in the form of a *double-entry journal*. The double-entry journal is one of an array of simple but effective literacy development tools meant to help facilitate reading comprehension and reflection. Ricci has asked students to copy five quotations they consider significant in the left column of a two-column page; the right-hand column is reserved for their own required commentaries and questions. Gabriel, for instance, highlights the Dubois maxim, "Ignorance is a cure for nothing," and responds philosophically on the right-hand side of the page: "I agree but it appears people in this society have not learned this—many would rather lead exciting lives full of drama than educate themselves. . . ."

The double-entry journals spark small-group discussion, which culminates with a written summary of the authors' main ideas on large chart paper suitable for whole-class viewing. After the small groups present the authors' views on education and progress of the "Negro race," Ricci asks each group to delineate similarities and differences on the charts, using a different color to underscore one or the other. Assuming they are well-prepared, and expecting productive effort, he exhorts them with a tight time limit: "You have 7 minutes!" The results are shared, discussed, and modified; Ricci periodically insists that students use direct evidence from the texts to support points made. In this fashion the students progress from comprehension to comparison, setting the stage for reflective historical analysis.

It is serious intellectual work, deliberately carried out. Students grapple with the task of differentiating the views of Dubois and Washington, gradually drawing powerful distinctions about their theories of social progress for an oppressed minority striving for social respect, status, and opportunity. The students' ideas coalesce with minimal help from Ricci, who takes on the role of commenting or asking questions based on discussion. They stress that Dubois has a more "top-down" or "trickle-down" philosophy, highlighting his emphasis on developing an intellectually enlightened and socially respected leadership—"the talented tenth"—and contrasting it with Washington's conviction that a "bottom-up" and labor-based approach, in which each one struggles for and earns a place in the industrial economy, is the means to progress. Theoretical and philosophical pondering gives way to biographical questioning. Students wonder about the influence of the authors' life experiences on their theories, thus bringing the relevance of point of view into stronger focus: "How did he [Dubois] become educated?" Students' values enter into their questioning as well, as they measure the relative merits of a focus on education to become "a better human" as compared to a "moneymaking machine."

Provocative questions about both philosophies get raised. "Who gets in the tenth?" one student asks. Will the top actually pull the bottom up? Will Whites provide the opportunity that Washington contends is mutually beneficial? Will the bottom still be seen as "lower"? These allusions to the climate of interracial tolerance and opportunity at the time lead to historical speculation. Questioning Washington's philosophy, one student suggests that the acquisition of money would not have led to "respect at that time," as compared to education; another counters that the education of Blacks might have been viewed by Whites as a threat. Earlier, one of the small groups had considered whether Dubois and Washington could have anticipated the civil rights accomplishments of the 1960s, and to what extent the development of their social theories was limited by historical experience at the turn of the century, not much more than a generation removed from the Civil War. But there is no time for Ricci to turn any of his students' momentary flirtations with the history of racial division, the African American struggle to overcome oppression, equality under the law, and equality of opportunity into teachable moments, and so further investigation of these themes and issues of historical context, continuity, and discontinuity must wait for another class.

Students conclude the hour having demonstrated substantial understanding of the texts and the theories of social betterment they represent, though they are not quite ready to say what they reflect in terms of social and intellectual history at the turn of the twentieth century. Most important, they were the primary authors of their understanding. Ricci structured the learning so that they had to introduce ideas to each other from the outset and collaborate in clarifying and expanding them. He did not lead the discussion, but framed it and then followed it, redirecting students at moments when they strayed from the evidence they had before them, a few times summarizing or adding briefly to what was said.

For many teachers, following and responding to students' thinking is counterintuitive pedagogy, an unnatural act. Feeling pressure to "cover" history, some may even equate their giving of information with their students learning it. Certainly there are junctures in the curriculum when students need critical background knowledge—time frames, events, key concepts, and personalities—in order to delve into a complex historical topic; Amy was providing a considerable amount to students who had never before considered "home" as a subject of historical inquiry. But a teacher who wants to stay true to the essential nature of history as a disciplined process of turning curiosity into inquiry, and the past into a treasure trove of messages about where we have been, who we are, and where we are going, must develop a pedagogy of active engagement in historical thinking, must strive to develop, in Ricci's words, "historical minds." That said, one must also calculate and support the trajectory of students' learning based on where they begin. Ricci is able to keep his scaffold of support relatively low—concentrating on framing the task, strategic questioning, and occasional summarizing—because students had higher levels of support during their previous 4-plus years at UPCS. He is able to minimize direction because of the norms and habits of learning that have been slowly ingrained, and which he reinforces.

Almost all of Ricci's students entered UPCS as seventh graders reading well below grade level. Most were unfamiliar with primary source analysis, and few if any would have been projected as AP students in other schools. They did not express, share, analyze, or develop subject matter ideas easily. But they were expected to be able to do so and to help each other in doing so, and were patiently taught how. They were given the opportunity to experience their own capability. Strategies calculated to foster academic development (e.g., literacy development in the form of double-entry journals), disciplinary aptitude (e.g., historical habits of mind in the form of Primary Source Circles), and competence in collaborative learning (e.g., in the collaborative structure of Primary Source Circles and interdependent small group work, as in Ricci's class) helped along the way.

In today's class students were unself-consciously and collaboratively engaged in their process of analysis; they *wanted* to figure out the differences between Dubois and Washington and willingly tried out their ideas on each other and their teacher. Whether aware of it or not, they were adhering closely to learning norms in the school culture, which had become increasingly natural. In fact, for them it was a routine day in the classroom.

LEARNING TO MAKE MORE FROM LESS WITH JESSE WEEKS

High expectations and rigorous content have merit as curriculum mantras, but they lose traction quickly in the classroom unless students' understanding of the workings of the discipline, belief in the value of what they are doing, and sense of efficacy in doing it are also carefully cultivated. Helping students understand how to learn history and why it is important is the challenge facing Ricci's colleague on the History Curriculum Team, Jesse Weeks, for 5 years a ninth-grade teacher of world history at South High and a graduate of the university teacher preparation program.

Jesse's starting point is different from Ricci's. Ricci's students arrive in his 11th-grade classroom with historical minds already engaged, but most of Jesse's arrive on the fault line separating academic and social insecurity and confidence. Unlike Ricci's, they have not had several years of socialization in the same tightly woven learning culture, with its consistent academic expectations and dedication to college readiness. Their transition to ninth grade—pivotal for many students in terms of persevering and achieving in school—therefore follows a steeper path; they must navigate a new social and academic environment, and adjust to new rules, demands, uncertainties, and pressures, as well as hopes. The trajectory of their development as history learners likewise begins at a more basic level. The challenge of providing the right scaffold for this development becomes a central issue in Jesse's day-to-day decision making.

The following question suggests the nature of Jesse's task: How do you engage academically underprepared students, making the transition from middle school to high school, in developing as critical readers, writers, and thinkers in history while meeting the many curriculum standards imposed by state and local guidelines? But the challenge facing Jesse is more complex. There is, first of all, the problem of time: It is virtually impossible to reconcile the curricular pace that Jesse must keep to conform to the standards with the time-intensive effort necessary to develop students' confidence and capabilities together with their understandings. Then there is the question of content itself. In the ossified condition in which it is presented in the state curriculum standards, historical content gives little indication of the hidden dynamic that formed it and that makes it alive and relevant; instead, another dynamic takes hold. To put it in its bleakest, barest form: The greater the number of standards, the greater the pressure of time to cover them, the more static and full of empty facts the content becomes, and the more disenchanted students become with history. And this dynamic affects underprepared and underperforming students the most, because they have the greatest difficulty keeping up with the unforgiving pace. Paradoxically, a supersaturated history curriculum can become an unwitting handmaiden to impoverished teaching—leading to a classroom full of repetitive tasks and worksheets that reduce learning to a mind-numbing exercise.

The antidote is not a simple matter of reducing the number of standards, although debating how many and which ones is a critical starting point. Ricci, Jesse, and many of our colleagues would certainly advocate for streamlining the curriculum to emphasize broad themes, each with sets of critical topics, questions, and a variety of sources that can be examined in some depth, with choice and flexibility in terms of timing put in the hands of teams of teachers at the school level. The depth and challenge of the curriculum would increase as students grow more capable and sophisticated in their historical reading, writing, and thinking.

But knowing how to make more out of less is equally vital. As Ricci's experience at UPCS suggests, the scaffold that teachers like Jesse must build for their students requires considerable disciplinary, pedagogical, and content knowledge and reflection, as well as support within the professional and student learning culture of the school. And the process must be cumulative, building from one teacher and grade to the next. The cornerstone of this effort is an insistent faith in students' capabilities that will enable them to develop belief in themselves.

Today Jesse is working with his "college-level" class. In district parlance college level refers to the lowest of three levels used to distinguish academic groups in high school, below the "honors" level and the highest level, "advanced placement." College level is meant to denote a college preparatory curriculum based on the same state standards that apply to all students, part of the effort to convey equity and greater uniformity in expectations. The idea of levels was introduced to replace the comprehensive high school tracks that had previously stratified students based on different expectations, standards, and outcomes. These three levels were reduced from the four in place before the district's major 5-year restructuring initiative supported by the Carnegie Corporation's "Schools for a New Society" program that ended in 2006.

The semantic and structural changes have symbolic importance. But by themselves they do not engender the fundamental changes in teaching practice and learning culture needed to dissolve the legacy of tracking at schools like South, which was complicated in South's history by rapid demographic changes in the 1980s and 1990s. When South endeavored to form small learning communities as part of the districtwide restructuring initiative, the founding teachers of the Information Technology Academy understood the subversive potential of this legacy: how indeed to prevent levels from becoming a new form of tracking defined by different academic expectations and different kinds of intellectual work? They did not trust that common state and district curriculum standards would result in equitable opportunity and learning across levels. They insisted, therefore, on a single-level system, making all classes heterogeneous; but, unlike UPCS, they did not designate these classes honors-level. Instead, students were given the opportunity to achieve honors by completing challenging assignments above and beyond the normal curriculum. Underprepared students were provided extra support, in the form of additional classes in literacy or mathematics. Their start-up philosophy had a strong parallel with UPCS, but they lacked the structural advantages of a Grades 7–12 school; they did not have the opportunity to induct students into a common learning culture and build their readiness for rigorous work beginning in the seventh and eighth grades.

Jesse is in the Arts and Humanities Academy of South High. This academy retains the three academic levels, in part to accommodate a group of designated "Goddard scholar" students that form in middle school and continue through high school. Although the levels remain, extra support for students in the form of a flexible seminar class focused on literacy, numeracy, and academic needs has been introduced in the ninth-grade program in an effort to equalize opportunity across the levels. Scheduling conflicts burden this effort, however, preventing Jesse and colleagues on his academy's ninth-grade team—the English, mathematics, biology, and special needs teachers—from getting together to assess student needs and plan how to take advantage of the seminar's potential to meet them; three of the four academic teachers, Jesse included, have responsibilities outside the team. Compounding their challenge, two of Jesse's colleagues, the English and mathematics teachers, do not teach the seminar at all, because the seminar adds to a teacher's workload according to the terms of the teachers' contract, and both colleagues are at the allowable number of five classes per day. Institutionalizing the seminar thus raises a concern about whether there are enough teachers for the increased number of classes. This concern, in turn, triggers questions about inflating class sizes to reduce the number of classes that need to be taught, or limiting the number of academic classes available to students, not to mention a threadbare budget. Efforts to develop a tight-knit culture of learning for Jesse's ninth-grade students and their teachers get caught in a web of trade-offs spun by competing needs, priorities, and limited resources.

As he notes in the background section of his Round sheet, Jesse's class has 18 students, about half the original enrollment; it is now April and the class was split in March, easing his management concerns and allowing him "to spend more time on teaching." Indeed, it is hard to imagine many more than 18 students in the small partitioned corner space available to him. Even with its reduced size, the class poses an array of challenges, as 12 of his students have Individual Learning Plans (5 of whom are formally classified as special needs students) and almost half read at a low-elementary level. The class is divided equally between students of color and White students. No matter whether it is large or small, underprepared or ready, the "class has been forced to move through content at an exceptional pace" as a result of state curriculum frameworks and district expectations.

Jesse silently bargains with the pressure to keep abreast of the district curriculum schedule, trying to do a little less and gain a little more in the process. Like Ricci, he combines literacy development with disciplinary tools and habits of mind in his teaching, routinely using writing prompts to elicit ideas, and primary sources to facilitate historical thinking. For most of his students the process is new: he spends a month at the beginning of the year familiarizing his college-level class with the characteristics of different kinds of primary and secondary sources and their use as tools in constructing historical understanding. Students gradually progress to learning the roles in primary source circles. At the time of the Round they are familiar with the roles of author and audience.

One of the ways Jesse eases his students into new norms of history learning is by using visual images. He has become adept at appealing to students' visual acuity, using works of art, posters, or other images as historical artifacts, often as a starting point for examining social issues—for example, social stratification as depicted in an ancient Egyptian frieze. Visual artifacts are valuable learning tools for all students, but increase the accessibility of content and open the door of inquiry in particular for English language learners or underprepared students still learning to decipher complex texts. Jesse often projects an image onto the whiteboard in his room, asking students what they notice. Everyone can notice something in a picture, point out what they see, and raise questions about what it is or why it is there; everyone can be involved. He highlights student observations on the projected image using colored whiteboard markers; the composite of these highlights sets in relief students' understanding of what is there, thus providing a vivid basis for discussing ideas about why it is there and what it means. Jesse usually combines images with written primary sources, which he shortens and edits as necessary, taking into account his students' progress in using reading strategies to understand challenging texts. He tries to keep the level of difficulty of a text within reach of the students without losing intellectual contact with the source as a whole.

Jesse's Round combines a content focus on "the use of propaganda as a tool to pass laws, reaffirm racist stereotypes, and justify war" during World War II with an examination of primary sources, one text-based, the rest visual. Today, rather than examine the sources as a whole class, Jesse structures three primary source stations, giving students a new measure of independence. At one table replicas of U.S. war posters exploit gross stereotypes of Japanese soldiers to stoke American fears and intensify munitions productivity on the home front. On another sits Jesse's laptop computer, playing an 8-minute cartoon video: a slapstick, Disney-generated contrast of American freedom and Nazi totalitarianism as seen from the perspective of Donald Duck. The third station displays colored drawings from a simple German children's picture book titled *A Poisonous Mushroom*. The text of the book is contained on a single page, translated from the German. Compared to the other examples of propaganda, the picture book seems innocent and inoffensive; these qualities make it all the more diabolical and also, as it turns out, challenging to understand.

Jesse assigns students to the three stations in groups. They will rotate from one to the other in three 8–10 minute intervals; their task is to examine the artifacts, and answer questions Jesse has provided on individual recording sheets. Each recording sheet begins by asking students to list some of the things they notice, following their usual protocol for examining artifacts. Students then fill in a simple T-chart, one side for inferences about some aspect of the artifacts, the other for evidence supporting the inferences—also a familiar learning practice. Jesse encourages students to share their observations with each other at the stations if time allows. In the final whole-group discussion they will focus on the framing question for the investigation: "What types of propaganda are most effective and why?"

Among the three stations, the posters draw the quickest response, students writing rapidly. The cartoon video, its elongated message unfolding gradually and requiring that students distinguish the comic scenes from their serious intent, collects a group of concentrated faces in front of the computer screen; it is their first effort to view a video as a primary source. Jesse perceives quickly that he needs to monitor the station with *The Poisonous Mushroom* most closely, as students try to fit the pictures and text together as if they were intricate puzzle pieces; in the next two rotations he decides to read the text aloud with students.

Two moments are emblematic of the myriad small ways in which opportunities for learning appear at any given point in a classroom, depending on what teachers ask students to do and how they interact with them in the process. One student excitedly seeks confirmation from Jesse that the symbols on a war poster—a swastika superimposed on a stylized glaring red sun—represent both Germany and Japan. The visual symbols attract his interest, the task chosen and constructed in a way that allows him to meet its challenges; Jesse's role is happily reduced to affirmation.

Jesse must respond much differently to the many students who labor over the text and corresponding pictures from *The Poisonous Mushroom*, calculating how best to support each student's process of understanding. The picture book describes a mother's simplistic instruction of her blond-haired little boy in the moral analogy between good and bad mushrooms and good and bad people. The analogy is stretched with a leap of racist logic that is not troubling to a very young boy anxious to please his mother: the moral of the story is that Germans are good, but Jews are comparable to poisonous mushrooms. The anti-Semitism is blatant, but not all students detect it immediately, and one hardworking student misses it entirely. It would be easy to correct her misreading, but much better of course to consider why it might have occurred and to help her see it on her own. Perhaps she cannot reconcile ethnic discrimination with a children's story, making it difficult for her to see any malignant irony in the bucolic watercolor of the mother and son picking mushrooms in the woods. Perhaps she reads only the first part of the story, compares it to the drawing, and concludes wrongly that the rest must be consistent. Or perhaps she is so intent on finishing her observation sheet—on completing the task set by the teacher—that she looks for answers to Jesse's questions rather than reading critically. It is at this point that a teacher has options that bear on the possibilities for her learning: to ask her what in the story led to her conclusion; to point out a statement in the story that conflicts with her own understanding; to ask her to reread the text, checking whether her understanding holds up; or to compare her interpretation with another student's. In this case, with encouragement, she rereads the end of the story and begins to see the conflict between her interpretation and the mother's closing statement that "Jews . . . are poison . . . and a solitary Jew can destroy . . . even the entire German people."

Visual and textual literacy are complementary, but obviously differ. Even among able readers, reading a text can be a complicated affair, because along with our ability to comprehend words, sentences, text, and tone, we bring our preconceptions and social constructions about form and substance, and they shape and filter our understandings. And visual and textual analysis combined, as in the case of the children's book, may pose additional challenges, as it seems to have done in the case of one of Jesse's students. It may take time for some students to sort through their meanings and make comparative sense of them.

Post-Round discussion focuses on Jesse's central goal of enabling students to analyze the propaganda and its effectiveness in light of the historical context. Jesse wishes he had spent more time during his introduction revisiting the process of examining a visual as well as textual primary source. He considers briefly whether a whole class format rather than stations might have allowed him to prepare students better for their examinations of the videotape and children's book. Attention turns to the effectiveness of the recording sheet questions in promoting analytical thinking. Jesse discusses the idea of streamlining the sheet so that students progress in one step from identifying what they notice to defining the propaganda message and identifying the evidence that supports it, rather than listing inferences and evidence and tackling several more questions. Jesse believes that the requirement of a longer written response would encourage students to explain their thinking more fully. Based on these observations, he decides to ask students to consolidate their understandings by writing a letter to an historian that explains the historical meaning of one of the artifacts, using the information gathered from their work at the stations.

Historical thinking is no more a natural and inevitable development than the ability to read different kinds of texts critically or write intelligently and fluently or, more generally, to handle "rigorous" work on the path to college readiness. These are all learned processes. To involve all students in them requires knowing how to make more from less: requires that they become embedded in the learning culture and curriculum; requires that the schedule is flexible, providing the extra time and personalized support that different students may need; and requires that teaching practice as a matter of course builds academic capability and confidence in concert with content understanding. Consider the inquiry process introduced by Amy, the conceptual analysis facilitated by Ricci, and the beginning steps toward critical examination supported by Jesse: They were fueled by intriguing historical artifacts grounded in the lives of real people, by significant questions about them that bear some relationship to our own lives, and by precious opportunities for thoughts to form, gain expression, confront evidence, and mature.

Curriculum policy often runs on the false principle that we get more if we include more or go faster or do everything the same. By contrast, making more from less seems the surer way to expand learning opportunity and enhance quality of learning for all students. Making more from less means making history a more authentic, textured, and enlivening learning process. It means, therefore, making the relationship between student and subject matter more intimate: opening up the inner workings of the subject so as to open up and engage student minds more fully, harnessing their curiosity, interests, and imagination; so as to draw students into particular worlds of the past to the extent that they begin to see them somewhat in their own terms. Making more from less opens minds and subject matter wide enough to increase the chance that students will see the relevance of history for themselves and analyze and articulate meaningful connections to the present. That would potentially enlarge their sense of human connectedness within and across time; their capacity for empathy; their understandings of our culturally diverse world; values such as equality, human rights, and social justice; and the significance of wondering, asking questions, and reading, writing, and thinking well.

CHAPTER 10

Lessons from Main South

THE NAME "MAIN SOUTH" has a generic quality. Indeed, Main South could stand for dozens of similar neighborhoods in small cities like Worcester and in larger ones across the country. It is, however, a very particular and personal place for hundreds of students and their families. For some, forced into a restless mode of living for various reasons, it is a temporary home; for many it is the place that will define their childhoods and adolescent years and will always be associated with them. How students will remember their young lives in Main South will depend on a range of factors. What role their schooling will play in turning their hopes and possibilities into opportunity and educational accomplishment, whether their futures—like those of Darius, Chau, and Kim—will turn more on their cultivated capability and the promise of education for everyone than on circumstance or chance, may well depend on whether teaching and their learning cultures develop along the path traveled by Kate, Adelina, Jody, Chris, Chad, Ricci, Jesse, and their likeminded colleagues.

What do we learn about what makes a difference for students from the practice of these Main South teachers? I revisit several topics in this concluding chapter: the nature and development of teaching quality—of an equitable and enabling teaching practice; the importance of coherent learning cultures based on principles of equity, personalization, literacy development, meaningful achievement, college readiness, and teacher collaboration; the value of the university partnership in fortifying teaching practice and expanding learning opportunity; and the closely related importance of policy initiatives that build the capacity for developing practice, support powerful learning cultures, and forge neighborhood-focused partnerships in our cities.

TEACHING QUALITY: EQUITY AND EFFECTIVENESS IN PRACTICE

As different as they are in terms of their subject matter, their school cultures, and their stages of professional development, Kate, Adelina, Jody, Chris, Chad, Ricci, and Jesse travel the same path in terms of developing equity and effectiveness in their teaching. Above all, they orient their "inner" or "invisible" practice by similar beliefs and assumptions. They share a conviction about the inherent capabilities of their students and trust that under the right conditions students can realize them for themselves. They believe that this realization occurs most powerfully when students discover and develop ideas on their own; that students must have some opportunity to follow paths of learning that make sense to them, not paths prescribed or followed by someone else, and learn to back up their conclusions. They believe in the value and relevance of what they are teaching, and strive to make it valuable and relevant to their students. They view their classes as learning communities filled with social and democratic meaning. Their students' ethnic, cultural, and linguistic diversity and competencies, together with their different ways of thinking, become part of the learning process; students learn that they can learn from and with each other. They want their students to experience the power of an equitable and integrated community forged from mutual respect and support for learning, and to understand firsthand the potential of each student's contribution to enhance the learning of the rest.

While they acknowledge the challenges that many students face in their personal lives and the social dynamics that may press limits upon them, they do not accept or excuse underperformance (see Kate's "Shepardean Oath" in Chapter 4). Instead, they view those circumstances as a professional challenge and responsibility, strive to instill the same attitude in their students, and, when they can, address it in these terms with parents. They share one other overriding characteristic: They trust in themselves as well as in their students. As much as they may respect and orient their teaching to required standards, they do not lose sight of larger purposes and the importance of meaning, authenticity, reflection, creativity, imagination, inspiration, and inner desire in learning. They are not trapped in the paradox that diminishes education under the pressure to achieve testable and measurable results.

This basic belief system forms the cornerstone of opportunity in their classrooms; but it is challenging to uphold and put into practice. As we discussed my write-up of her teaching, Jody Bird, in her 8th year as a teacher, reflected that her practice has matured only recently to the point exemplified in her Round, in which she integrates critical dimensions of academic learning. Viewed comparatively and as a whole, their experiences suggest that they must master a variety of complex tasks with each group of students in order to develop their teaching along these lines. I have broadly characterized and arranged the tasks in Figure 10.1 to suggest the general path the teachers must travel. In practice the stages are more blurred and interrelated than implied by this model of development.

In the formative and equitable stages of Figure 10.1, as Adelina, Chad, Chris, and Jesse would attest, their beliefs place a burden on their teaching to engender a level of trust with their students in the face of their fears, re-sistance, reluctance, or sense of failure, low status, disconnection, anxiety, or skepticism. They must find a way to tap into their students' desire to believe in themselves and to have someone believe in them. They must help students to recognize and trust their intellectual and academic capabilities and the value of developing them: Everyone is a reader, writer, and thinker. They must find accessible, meaningful, and mind-opening ways for students to enter into and explore subject matter, and corresponding ways to check for and help them refine their thinking. They must help students form social as well as personal habits of learning that respect individual thinking and build mutual understanding. Opportunity expands as they provide students with curriculum material that entices their emotional as well as intellectual involvement, and that challenges them at the perceived limit of their capa-bility. It grows as students begin to trust and take on the identities as learn-ers that their teachers affirm in them.

Opportunity and equity expand further as the teachers develop their fa-cility in making more from less. They balance high expectations with scaf-folding that builds their students' capabilities as readers, writers, and think-ers. They do not confuse a rigorous and meaningful curriculum with one operating on the principle that more and faster is better. They open minds by opening up and thereby slowing down the curriculum and content, so as to allow room for different points and modes of entry and depth of learn-ing. They make sure that their students experience their ability to explore, develop, analyze, and present ideas, and to mature habits of mind while practicing the active ways in which knowledge is produced in a discipline. They elevate both the floor and ceiling of achievement for all students. Most students are beginning to think of themselves as writers, or at least to un-derstand the value of writing in the development of their thinking and as an expression of themselves worth sharing. Most consider themselves as young scientists, mathematicians, historians, and literary readers, laying the groundwork for understanding how formal knowledge is developed and put to use in society. Most understand that they are capable of postsecondary learning, that what they are doing in their classes is preparing them for it, that it is important for them.

Yet their teachers understand that each of them may need a different kind and/or degree of support in the process. They recognize that small but important opportunities for learning are often created or lost depending on the teacher's attentive eye and reflective conscience, depending on what a teacher learns from what a student reveals about his or her own thinking and inner world and what a teacher confronts in his or her own thinking, and depending on the actions that follow. So they pay close attention to what students are thinking, what they are able to do, and what puzzles, confounds, perplexes, or intrigues them; the Rounds process of collaboration sharpens this attentive care. In due course, they pay attention to their own uncertainties, questions, and concerns about a student, turn them into momentary inquiries, and develop new strategies of support.

The teachers also personalize and enact equity in their practice through community. Elizabeth Cohen (1994), a sociologist who studied the impact of social status in the classroom on performance, emphasized that each student is capable of contributing to the learning of the others in a variety of ways that should be recognized and utilized in the learning process; each has competence that classmates should know about and value. Teachers who publicly affirm a student's competence—for example, by assigning a particular role in group work—enhance that student's social standing and identity as a classroom learner, thus counteracting any inimical prejudices carried into the classroom from the outside. These Main South teachers publicly recognize and value each student's thinking, striving to appropriate it for the benefit of the learning of all. They model a social process of learning in which respecting, sharing, checking, and connecting individual thinking is a habitual activity, and one in which every student can participate and have some measure of agency. They bring students together regularly for this purpose, in pairs or small groups formed on the basis of nonacademic as well as academic strengths, taking into account personality, facility with language and communication, social skills, literacy development, academic capabilities, and confidence. In this way they strive to make thinking visible and learning transparent, to equalize status, and to make responsibility for learning communal.

At the transformative level their teaching is multidimensional and integrated, reflecting the ecology of academic learning represented in Jody's practice. They regularly combine content learning focused on conceptual understanding with participation in the disciplinary way of knowing (with an emphasis on habits of mind and learning), the development of academic capability (with a focus on academic literacy), personalization, and learning community. Over time, academic learning for their students becomes purposeful and integrated as well. This formulation sounds much simpler than it is, however; it is not more prevalent partly because achieving it is inherently a demanding process and partly because a system based on strict curriculum standards and schedules, and timed, test-based results, however well-intentioned, does not directly support it. For beginning teachers, the task may appear nearly impossible, with periods of seeming progress counteracted by bewildering setbacks.

Even with the resolve and determination shown by teachers like Adelina, Chad, Chris, and Jesse, the support and perspective of others, such as those participating in the professional learning community formed by the university partnership, can prove critical. Not only is the formation of their

Figure 10.1. Toward an Equitable and Transformative Practice

INNER PRACTICE	FORMATIVE PRACTICE	EQUITABLE PRACTICE	TRANSFORMATIVE PRACTICE
Reflective alignment of belief and purpose	**Key supports for powerful learning**	**Opportunity and personalized academic support for all students**	**Integrated academic learning**
Belief system *(assumptions about students, learning, and purposes)*	Trust and relationships	High expectations	Curriculum *(conceptual understanding)*
Self-trust and integrity	Curriculum *(accessible, mind-opening, meaningful core concepts; purposeful, connective, engaging)*	Curriculum *(make more from less)*	Disciplinary habits *(disciplinary habits of mind and learning)*
Reflection *(examining and coordinating belief, purpose, and action)*		Personalization *(attentiveness, inquiry, assessment, scaffolding)*	Academic capability *(academic literacy)*
Empathy and inquiry *(understanding students and their learning)*	Academic identities *(all students are readers, writers, and thinkers)*	Learning community *(equal status, mutual support and commitment, multiple ways of thinking, shared habits, and transparency in learning)*	Personalization
	Learning community *(norms and habits of collaborative learning)*		Learning Community
			Integrated reflection and inquiry

practice and the learning experience of their students at stake, but also the emotional, intellectual, and vocational sustenance they need if they are to remain in the profession. Jody, Kate, and Ricci, the most experienced teachers in the Main South group, each with at least 7 years in the classroom, have developed their practice so that it has transformative capability. While it might have grown similarly under different circumstances, given who they are, they have had the benefit of an extraordinarily conducive environment: a school with a single-minded mission embodied in the attitudes and practices of colleagues, principals who have valued and supported the collegial environment, and a like-minded university partner; a culture that values continuous sharing and learning, and facilitates it with collaborative learning practices such as Rounds, and in which teachers together assess student performance and strive to improve; an uplifting schoolwide sense of community. They teach in a culture with surpassing coherence and integrity, and a capacity for growth.

Richard Elmore (2003) asserts that "internal coherence around instructional practice is a prerequisite for strong [student] performance, whatever the requirements of the external accountability system" (p. 9). Jody, Kate, and Ricci exemplify internal coherence with the transformational components of their practice: their similar understanding of content goals (central concepts), disciplinary learning and habits of mind, literacy development, scaffolding and rigor, personalization and collaborative learning in their classrooms.

Although Adelina, Chad, Chris, and Jesse, as active members of the partnership learning community, are committed to developing their practice guided by these same principles and values, they do not have the advantage of doing so in comparable school cultures. Instead, they simultaneously face the challenges of their own practice as teachers at an early stage in their careers and the particular needs of the redeveloping cultures at their schools. Neither school history nor policy is of particular help to them. Whereas UPCS was cast in the mold of a neighborhood school dedicated to preparing students for college, their schools endeavor to refocus and rebuild cultures that were conceived much differently. Even as they strive to develop their teaching practice in line with a mission of college readiness, their schools must cast off conflicting historical purposes and practices and set a course for change against the headwinds of a system of accountability pressing so hard for quicker, better results that teaching itself can lose a sense of bearing, can become one-dimensional, defensive, and ultimately uninspired. It is as challenging under these circumstances for them to maintain integrity, focus, and hope in their practice as it is for their schools to establish a new cultural coherence.

The opportunities for collaborative learning, knowledge exchange, and support provided through the university partnership help these teachers to maintain a common direction while in their different schools. As a group they represent many of these opportunities. Each of them has worked with at least one of the others outside her or his own school: Kate and Adelina work closely together as members of the Hiatt Center Mathematics Curriculum Team and have visited each other's classrooms; Jody's classroom was familiar to Chris as a Master of Arts in Teaching student; Ricci and Jesse have a common background as members of the History Curriculum Team; Chad knows the UPCS teachers, since he was an MAT there. They all have the same supportive colleagues at the university. Clark University plays a role that is needed, and one that can be filled by other universities as part of a concerted effort to ensure the development of teaching quality as a central goal of reform.

Comparable opportunities and support are needed for their schools. Adelina, Chad, Chris, Jesse, and their colleagues need time for common planning and for engaging regularly in collaborative learning practices, such as Rounds, which keep them focused on realizing a shared and prioritized set of principles, values, and goals in their practice and their students' academic development. Their schools need flexibility in enacting new ideas, and the opportunity to hire, if not to help prepare—as in the Master of Arts in Teaching program supported by the partnership between their schools and the university—teachers who will fully participate in and nurture the new culture.

The more general lesson to draw from the experience of these teachers is that reform, teacher development, and knowledge exchange need to be contextualized within broader systems of support. The historical and cultural backgrounds of schools are different and must be taken into account in the effort to cultivate learning cultures and teaching quality that ensure and elevate the accomplishment of all students. Teachers need systems of support within schools, partnerships, and inter-school or cross-school networks that facilitate a collaborative process of developing and sharing knowledge about practice that cultivates the academic capability of all students.

TOWARD A TRANSFORMATIVE LEARNING CULTURE: THE EXAMPLE OF UNIVERSITY PARK CAMPUS SCHOOL

What does an equitable and transformative coherence in culture and practice look like at the school level? What are some of the developmental benchmarks on the way to establishing this coherence? Even as Jody, Kate, and Ricci share teaching principles and values that cut across their different grade levels and subject areas, their practice represents a broader, mission-driven coherence at UPCS. Each enacts a basic stage in an expected and planned trajectory of academic development from middle school learning to college-ready learning. In other words, each of them helps fulfill a cross-grade curriculum designed to guide students, in particular the low-performing students who enter the school, to progressively higher levels of academic capability and confidence through their 6 years of learning.

The UPCS educational culture is fashioned from whole cloth—coherence and integrity run deep and long. Just as teachers like Jody, Kate, and Ricci learn to weave together critical dimensions of teaching and academic development into a strong narrative of equitable learning in their practice, the school as a whole has evolved in understanding how to fulfill its mission so that the narrative builds coherently from one grade to the next, and through the transition to college. Structure, curriculum, learning culture, and teaching practice, as well as partnership practice, form from mission, beliefs, and commitments, engendering a powerful sense of purpose and experience of community. Although expectations are high, they do not burden the culture unduly with performance pressure, as they might elsewhere; rather, the high expectations bind teachers together and, over time, students as well. This is a challenge of reform that the school and its university partner meet: to balance insistent high expectations, a demanding and engaging curriculum, and focused purpose with a sense of shared responsibility, mutuality, and personal support for academic development. Teachers and students on the whole take a positive, developmental view; the aim above all is for students to believe and become more fully what they already are, not to measure what they are not. The narrative life of the school, reinforced by the university partnership, follows from this educational premise. Most students willingly take their part in the archetypal story played out there, in which they overcome any limiting social or personal expectations, meet challenges, support one another, and begin to realize their capabilities as learners and human beings.

Structurally, the small size of UPCS and 6-year grade span are advantageous, but only because of how the school utilizes the particular capacity these characteristics provide to build unity in mission and coherence in practice and culture, to foster academic development, and to establish a culture of personalization as well as achievement (see Table 10.1). Small schools caught fire over the past decade as a breakthrough model of reform. Yet by no means are they a panacea; merely scaling down does not guarantee big results.

Recent research has explored the relationship of size to student performance and questioned whether small size matters more for underperforming students. One study finds that a range of 600–900 students is optimal, but many schools, such as UPCS, choose a lower threshold (Lee & Smith, 2001). Studies tend to concur on the positive impact small size has on the social as well as academic environments of schools, on their beneficial effect on student attendance, interpersonal relationships, commitment, achievement, and 4-year graduation rates (Jacobowitz, Weinstein, Maguire, Luekens, & Fruchter, 2007). But there are cautions, as factors such as the academic skills of entering students and lack of cohesion in the "pedagogical as well as non-academic domains of a school," may militate against high performance (Jacobowitz et al., 2007, pp. 34–35). On balance, the evidence strongly favors a small school, in particular for poor students for whom achievement historically has been problematic, but only if the opportunities afforded by a compact size are appreciated and used well, as illustrated in the case of UPCS.

The small-school literature gives less attention to the potential advantages of a middle to high school grade span. But the study of high-performing versus low-performing small Grades 9–12 schools in New York City by Jacobowitz et al. (2007) suggests indirectly that a longer developmental period might benefit schools challenged to support students who enter as underperformers. More time with these students—assuming that other critical factors in the learning environment, such as cohesiveness in organization and instructional practice, are in place—might enhance the opportunity for academic development. Certainly this is the experience at UPCS.

Whether or not a wider grade span is adopted, schools need flexibility in their schedules and curricula to develop an academic program that matches the needs of students: longer periods, supplemental periods, combined periods, an after-school homework center—these are all in the mix at a school like UPCS. Schools need a similar flexibility in accountability: flexible testing schedules based on student development (if testing must be used), alternative performance measures such as portfolios that illustrate academic development and align with state college entrance requirements, attention to graduation and college-going rates.

Broken into its developmental parts, the culture of postsecondary readiness at UPCS becomes a series of distinct goals and curricular stages (see Table 10.1). The school conceives the middle school years, Grades 7–8, as a period of formation in preparation for the "honors" curriculum in which all students will enroll in ninth grade. Students are grouped heterogeneously. Their daily schedule includes four core academic classes (English language arts, history, mathematics, and science) and an additional class in which literacy, numeracy and other academic skills are taught, based on individual student needs; once a week they will have physical education at the university athletic center, and a class in art, music, health, or Shakespeare. The schedule maximizes instructional time; all of the classes last for at least an hour, and several for 75 minutes.

Teachers make more from less. During their first two years students learn the norms and expectations of learning at the school, in particular the importance of taking responsibility for their work and of respecting and learning to collaborate with others. They begin to think of themselves as literary readers, as young mathematicians, scientists, and historians, as writers and thinkers. They build academic capability—with an emphasis on learning how to comprehend different kinds of texts and express ideas in writing—and algebraic thinking. Mindful of the importance of preparing students for their transition into the school, this learning process begins before school starts, during a 3-week summer "academy" which combines several hours of daily academic work with recreation. The goal of the academy is to ensure that all students enter the school believing in themselves as readers, writers, and mathematical thinkers, and knowing that they are beginning their preparation for college. The summer academy teachers, including Kate, will continue teaching the incoming seventh graders for the next 2 years, thus building relationships, trust, and closeness as a cohort group. And, like their colleagues in the upper grades, they will work together as a team to assess and support individual student progress. These features of the middle school program ensure strong continuity and coherence in goals, curriculum, teaching practice, personalization, and learning experience.

The students enter a more content-rich and demanding curriculum beginning in ninth grade. Signifying a new beginning, teachers immerse students in a second transitional summer academy. But this is a recent addition

Table 10.1. Academic Development and Coherence at University Park Campus School

Key Areas	Stages of Academic Development Leading to College Readiness (Cross-Grade Curriculum)				
	Grades 7–8	Grade 9	Grades 10–11	Grade 12	Postsecondary
Mission	Develop capabilities and confidence as readers, writers, and thinkers. Begin learning habits of mind and learning typical of literary readers, historians, mathematicians (all students algebra ready), and scientists. Prepare for rigorous coursework in 9th grade.	Continue to form academic capabilities and identities; develop habits of mind and learning. Build capacity to do challenging work, read sophisticated texts, write clearly and persuasively. Master core content concepts.	Same as Grade 9.	Same as Grades 9–11. Develop "college readiness"—prepare students for the modes of learning and expectations of college. Guide students through the college application process.	Support graduates through postsecondary transition.
Structure	Small size, 35–40 students per grade. All classes are on first floor, near principal's office.	Small size, 35–40 students per grade.	Same as Grade 9.	Same as Grades 9–11.	Alumni meetings, surveys, and networks.
Curriculum/ Learning Culture	A 3-week summer academy immerses students in reading, writing, and thinking across the curriculum and assesses their academic preparedness. Core academic classes (long periods) and supplemental academic skills class (literacy, numeracy, study skills). Weekly classes in art, music, physical education. State curriculum standards are followed. Before- and after-school homework center.	All classes are honors level. A 3-week summer 9th grade transition Academy immerses students in an interdisciplinary field-based research project and new expectations for learning. Curriculum follows state standards for each discipline. Students heterogeneously grouped. At least one Advanced Placement (AP) option. Before- and after-school homework center.	Heterogeneous honors classes. Long class periods in English language arts and mathematics in 10th grade. Qualified 11th graders take a University course. AP options. Before- and after-school homework center. Students and parents meet with alumni and university staff to discuss college readiness. Internship and community service opportunities.	Students take several classes structured like traditional college courses, requiring more independent work and self-monitoring. Semester-long electives in science and social sciences. Qualified students take a university course; others audit them. Seminar guides students in college application process. Sessions with alumni.	Matriculating students are connected to alumni who attend their colleges.

Table 10.1. (*continued*)

Teaching Practice	Teachers spend 2 years with each cohort of students (looping). Teachers focus on academic capability, community expectations and habits of learning, and habits of mind. Same teachers in English language arts, math, science, history for both grades. Teachers share knowledge on individual student needs and progress (data analysis). Rounds.	Integrate literacy development, conceptual learning, and habits of mind. Increase challenge levels. Emphasize personal responsibility. Teachers collectively assess and make decisions on how to support student progress; conduct data analysis. Rounds.	Same as Grade 9.	Same as Grades 9–11. In addition, expose students to different methods they might encounter in college, including a combination of lecture/lab work or lecture/reading discussion group.	
Partnership Support/College Socialization	P.E. classes on campus. Access to university library. Volunteers for homework center. Graduate teacher interns. Collaborative learning practices.	Mentor program to support UPCS students. Academic seminars. Collaborative learning practices. Graduate teacher interns.	Same as Grade 9. Also opportunity for university courses.	Same as Grades 9–11. Also opportunity for Clark University courses and courses at other nearby colleges.	Dedicated advisor for matriculating UPCS students.

to the curriculum. Concerned about the discrepancy between their expectations for student performance and the students' expectations for themselves, the ninth-grade teachers decided that they needed some form of common experience that would set the tone and direction for the learning community for the year. This summer academy program casts students as young researchers and scholars, and inducts them into the world of knowledge making and the thinking process and responsibilities it entails. The program is team-taught, interdisciplinary, and driven by a unifying theme. The first academy program was titled "A Sense of Place: Evolving Land Use in New England." Students discovered their urban living space anew, as they examined the relationship between the human and natural environments in their neighborhood and just beyond. The curriculum involved collaborative field-based research; stressed inquiry, data gathering, analysis, and reflection as habits of mind; and culminated in student presentations. Several experiences blended community building with field investigation, as students and teachers went canoeing and hiking together, within and just outside the confines of the city. The habits of mind resonated in the curriculum for the remainder of the year, together with habits of learning that include taking responsibility, collaborating, and persisting—rethinking and revising as necessary—in order to attain quality in their work.

As 10th graders, UPCS students have longer class periods in English language arts and mathematics, partly in deference to the statewide tests in those subjects that they will take at the end of the year. But the stress on conceptual understanding and learning what it means to be literary readers, historians, mathematicians, and scientists remains the same and will continue for the duration of their academic learning at the school. As 10th and 11th graders they will be challenged to take advantage of opportunities to test and stretch their academic prowess. Some students will participate in the weekly seminars occasionally offered by a university professor. Others will choose the Advanced Placement option open to any student, meeting for extra class sessions as some do in U.S. history with Ricci Hall. Many of these same students will strive to earn the support of their teachers for taking an introductory level course at Clark University in 11th grade; about half will before they graduate. Beyond the academic, they will be given opportunities for community-based internships and service, an extension of the curriculum designed to expose them to professional environments and to give them experience in taking responsibility in different settings.

The 12th-grade curriculum marks yet another distinct shift in academic development—to college transition. It is a work in progress, evolving as all concerned learn from recent graduates what makes the difference in their postsecondary readiness, perseverance, and accomplishment. There are academic as well as nonacademic components, reflecting the distinct needs of

first-generation college-going students whose families may have little procedural knowledge of the college application and selection process, and who
will be expected to navigate a new social and cultural terrain, sometimes
with minimal on-site support and guidance. Here are key elements to date
of the culminating year curriculum:

- Students choose among several electives in the sciences and social
  sciences.
- Students take several courses structured and taught according to a
  traditional college model. The courses are semester-long, use syllabi,
  and require students to complete some readings and assignments on
  their own; if they need help, they need to solicit it for themselves. A
  science course might combine 3 days of lectures with independent
  reading and a long lab session; social science courses might combine
  lectures with a discussion group based on assigned weekly readings.
  Although the teaching models mimic traditional college formats,
  students are aware of the safety net provided by teachers who know
  and care for them; their teachers, however, give them more leeway
  than in previous grades to learn from a failure to meet expectations
  and take responsibility for their own learning.
- Students who will not take a course at the university before they
  graduate must audit a university course for a 3-week period and
  visit the course instructor during his or her office hours to talk
  about the content of the course. The instructor signs off on the visit.
  This is part of the process of helping students learn how to find help
  when they need it and advocate for themselves, as well as tap into
  the intellectual life of a college environment.
- The Senior Seminar guides students through the various stages of
  the college selection process, beginning with identifying colleges that
  match interests and academic readiness, preparing the application,
  choosing which college to attend, and preparing for the transition.
  At a college awareness day students and parents hear from alumni
  and Clark University personnel on what to expect at college and
  what academic and nonacademic resources are available to help
  incoming students (faculty advisors, writing centers, math labs, the
  Dean of Students office, and so on).
- Finally, in the fall of their senior year, the school tries to determine
  which students will need to take a developmental or remedial course
  during their first year of college unless provided with additional
  support, based on the assessment used for students entering the
  state college system. As I note in Chapter 1 and in the data reported
  in Chapter 2's Appendix, this is a particular concern in college

readiness. Once identified, these students will receive extra help during the latter part of their senior year in an effort to obviate this transitional step, which delays and can discourage their assimilation into the credit-bearing curriculum.

By the time they graduate, students will know any UPCS alumni who are attending their colleges of choice, and who are beginning to form networks of mutual support. Once in college, they will be asked to help assess the value of the senior year program vis-à-vis their college preparation, and their progress will be tracked.

It is early to judge how much the reconceptualization of the senior year at UPCS is increasing students' understanding of college preparation and application, facilitating the transition to college, and ensuring retention and success. The preliminary data suggest a beneficial effect, as at least 80% of graduates from the past 2 years remain in college and are on track to finish within 6 years, a larger percentage than in previous classes, and far greater than the national norm.[1]

PARTNERSHIP COHERENCE AND INTEGRITY

It is difficult to measure the impact of the university partnership on practice, culture, coherence/integrity, academic development, and college readiness. But the presence of the university in the consciousness and activity of the school, and, indeed, the school in the consciousness and activity of the University, evident in many ways, suggest that together they create a new and powerful context for learning. The two have grown together, one year at a time since the opening of the school, each institutionally and, more important, culturally connected with the other. The academic and nonacademic opportunities given to students through the partnership, and the high rate of knowledge exchange and development fostered through collaborative professional learning and joint work on teacher preparation have proved to be the most significant agents of cultural crossbreeding.

Students understand that the cultural as well as physical geography of UPCS includes Clark University from their very first exposure to the school. During the seventh-grade summer academy they have recreational activities on campus. Eventually they will be introduced to the university library (founded in the 1880s as a small neighborhood elementary school, the UPCS building has no room for a library), athletic center, where they have their physical education classes, and campus center, which is often the site of special schoolwide events. By the time they are seniors all of the students will have attended, if not taken, a course on campus. Many of them will

have had a university student as a mentor in a program designed to cultivate college aspiration and socialization, with group activities on campus.
Some will have been tutored by a university student. Most will have been
taught by at least one of the five graduate teaching interns assigned there
each academic year.

Graduate teaching interns constituted half of the small teaching staff of
four at the school in its first year and have been a constant presence since.
Several of the current full-time teachers interned at the school; about two
thirds have a degree in education from Clark University. Most teachers take
part regularly with Hiatt Center staff, and occasionally with university arts
and sciences faculty, in one or more of the various forms of collaborative
learning that I have described. They all open their classrooms to visitors
from the university and beyond. This transparency reinforces community
values of trust, student-centeredness, collaboration, mutual support, and
growth. The resulting stream of interaction and dialogue powers an evolving understanding of what it means to put purpose into practice and to
teach all students well.

Partnership, too, can be mutually transformative. But, as the experience
of UPCS suggests, there are big "ifs"—if animated by openness, trust, unity
of purpose, dedicated leadership and a joint decision making process, stead-
fast institutional commitment, mutual appreciation, common practices and
goals, joint assessment, and a collaborative spirit. The UPCS partnership remains strong after more than a decade, the commitments entailed bolstered
by the heartening achievements of students. Yet there is still much to be
learned, in particular as the lives of students like Darius, Chau, and Kim un-
fold through college and beyond. How many students indeed will finish college? What will enable them and what will the achievement mean for them?
What will they later contribute? In what sense will their participation in the
educational narrative of their school give them lessons in equity, diversity,
community, and commonality that will serve them well in the communities
they will help form and sustain? How do the lessons of UPCS get appropri-
ated by others, in particular by schools with different histories and cultures?
How do we assess and sustain the work over time?

The partnerships with Claremont Academy and South High evolve in an
effort to support change toward a powerful coherence in culture and practice at these schools. Although they incorporate some of the same activities
that weave together the efforts of UPCS and the university, the partnerships
at their current stage of development are much less comprehensive and culturally embedded.

Claremont has incorporated a university mentor program for students
and academic seminars such as Amy Richter's (Chapter 9); a cohort of MAT
students have taught there; and teachers other than Adelina and Chad have

begun to participate in the partnership's professional learning community. Signs of the potential of the partnership to enrich the context of learning for students emerge: A Hiatt Center professor and pair of teachers collaborate on an interdisciplinary course for seniors to build their confidence to meet the intellectual rigors of college; rising sophomores and juniors express interest in qualifying to take courses at Clark University before they graduate.

The University's own limited capacity—for example, to offer course opportunities to high school students— and the challenge of converting a complex institutional structure and culture shorten the reach of the partnership at South High. The MAT internship program and the involvement of teachers like Jesse in collaborative learning activities remain the most prominent signs of the partnership. But there are promising developments. Recently, all of the teachers at South High, as well as those from Claremont, participated in a daylong series of teacher-led sessions, sponsored by the partnership, on the role of writing in learning. As a follow-up, small teams of teachers will meet at the university to map out concrete ways to use writing to enhance content learning.

EXPANDING THE CONTEXT OF LEARNING:
TOWARD AN EDUCATIONAL COMMUNITY

What road do schools like Claremont, South High, and UPCS, together with their university partner, need to travel on the way to an equitable and coherent culture and a powerful context for learning in their urban neighborhood? If we fold together the ideas about practice, academic development, and partnership represented in the experience of the Main South teachers and their schools, we might imagine a developmental scale such as that in Table 10.2. This scale is painted with very broad strokes, more a vista than a road map. It suggests a direction of travel and a horizon line, but it is also deceptively simple. The Main South experience makes clear that taking the journey means challenging convention, at least in terms of thinking what is possible and how to achieve it. It means moving past constraining beliefs and systems and possibly closing one chapter and writing a new one in a school's history. In partnership it means finding ways to learn together from different vantage points.

If there is one helpful overriding message in the face of these challenges, it may be to cast aside fear in putting belief into practice, to collaborate and trust sincerity of effort, to favor action over delay, and to be willing to learn in the process. One can imagine policies that support this movement: policies with incentives for change that build the capacity for coherence

Table 10.2. Developing School Coherence and Integrity

Domain	Critical Areas	Developmental Stages and Tasks		
		Formative	**Cohesive**	**Mature**
Mission		Establish mission that includes goal of postsecondary readiness.	Align curriculum, practice, and culture to mission.	Ensure that all activity aligns with and supports the fulfillment of mission.
School Structure	Size	Map out conversion from large to small.	Small and self-contained.	Small, personalized, communal.
Curriculum	Subject area	Connect content learning goals to disciplinary thinking and doing.	Make more from less. Incorporate academic capabilities and disciplinary habits in curriculum.	Integrate and assess in practice key concepts, understanding, disciplinary habits and academic development in curriculum.
	Grade level	Establish common expectations and goals. Implement fearlessly!	Incorporate gradewide habits of thinking, doing, and collaborating in practice.	Integrate and assess literacy development across the curriculum, common habits of mind, and common goals based on academic development.
	Developmental; cross-grade level	Establish a vision for stages of development.	Define and implement goals and practices for each stage.	Fully implement and assess a developmental, carefully staged curriculum leading to college readiness (academic, procedural, and social readiness).
Practice		**Formative**	**Equitable**	**Transformative**
Culture	Learning culture for students	Establish beliefs, expectations, and goals based on principles of equity, literacy, and academic development, and college readiness.	Ensure that all students learn in classes with similar expectations and equitable teaching and support.	Ensure that all students experience equality in status; that all value and have access to personalized academic support; that all participate in collaborative forms of learning.
	Learning culture for adults	Establish ways to learn and assess professional practice based on mission and student learning goals.	Implement practices to support individual teacher development and collaborative teacher planning and learning in relation to the expectations and goals for student learning.	Make teaching practice and assessment of student learning transparent; teachers routinely share and develop practice and inquire into student learning together. Principal/teachers set individual and group goals and support one another in achieving them. Functions, therefore, as a vocational rather than institutional community.
Higher Education Partnership	Academic support; teacher support and development; assessment.	Agreement on initial opportunities, goals, and practices in support of students and teachers. Establish coplanning and decision-making process.	Implement programs of academic support and enhancement, professional development, and knowledge exchange and collaborative learning.	Assess/develop programs that enhance academic curriculum and learning, knowledge exchange and collaborative learning, teacher development, and college understanding.

in mission, structure, curriculum, culture, practice, and readiness for post-secondary education; policies that likewise build equity integrity, that support the establishment of small-school partnerships, neighborhood-based and otherwise, with an opportunity to function and grow independently, and that bring together schools, universities, and new teacher development; policies with the leverage necessary for remaking education in places like Main South.

If we imagine more broadly, we might envision the possibility of a new context for learning and new educational narrative formed by schools, universities, and neighborhoods, if not an embracing and vital educational community. This community taps something essential in education: the power of learning to help us see, think, act, relate, and interact in more expansive, more understanding, and more deeply human ways; to explore and create new worlds; to make ourselves and our world better. I am reminded daily of the challenges of developing this kind of community, but more powerfully of its possibilities, mostly in small ways.

Just the other day, I saw two of Kim's younger sisters. They both were bouncing basketballs, not quite in unison, on a neighborhood jaunt to the university athletic center. We chatted for a few moments. Just graduated from UPCS, the older sister will attend Middlebury College in the fall, to study science, joining her brother there. Her younger sister made sure to tell me that her brother is studying English not science. She is a fourth grader in the elementary school that resides in the old South High building that once nurtured Robert Goddard's dreams on his way to advanced study at Clark University. These sisters are connected to the university, too, and the university to them.

And about 2 weeks ago, a Claremont ninth grader, stimulated by a short seminar given by a university professor at the school, told me about her interest in knowing more about attempts in her native country, Albania, to protect Jewish people during the Holocaust. We arranged a visit to the university's Strassler Center for Holocaust and Genocide Studies. She brought along a colorful entourage of seven other students, a group representing different cultural backgrounds and grades, and would have brought more if not for a conflict with a sports event. Several of these students want to take a course on the subject at the university. This was a small opportunity; but it fed the desire to know and opened a door to a larger world.

Even as it is beset with challenges, the current era of reform is rife with opportunity and hope. Darius, Kim, and Chau do not need to stand alone. Yet it will take concerted and committed action to overturn convention and turn opportunity and hope into a new reality of schooling, particularly in our cities. We can remake the culture of learning in schools provided that we refocus on establishing coherence in mission, academic programs, and practice. We can make teaching practice more powerful by strengthening and enlarging professional learning communities meant to support and sustain teachers, exchange and generate knowledge, and build individual and collective capacity to engage the mind and heart of each student and elevate the achievement of all. We can leverage the power of partnership in this process and create more community-centered approaches to change. By doing so, we will make learning more meaningful and connected to everyday life and hopes. And we will make democratic reform of our schools a concept alive with a conscience, a heart, and willing hands joined together.

Notes

Chapter 1

1. Many studies address the question of whether and how poverty impacts school readiness and performance. Perhaps most notable, the economist Richard Rothstein (2004) strongly questions whether patterns of low performance among low-income families can change fundamentally without a corresponding change in living conditions. David Berliner (2006) provides an incisive summary of the issue.

2. Hill, Campbell, and Harvey (2000) characterize one such approach as the "Community Partnerships strategy." Under this strategy "all the community's resources, not simply its schools, would be available in an organized way to meet children's educational needs and their general well-being" (p. 77).

3. The results noted by Berliner (2006) might be viewed instructively in terms of the sense of self-worth generated by a change toward greater equality in social status. Certainly a student's sense of social status in schools can make a difference in attitude and motivation, as I mention briefly in Chapter 10 of this volume in relation to Elizabeth Cohen's (1994) work. Michael Fullan (2006) notes the importance of one's perception of social status to success in his discussion of *The Impact of Inequality* (2005) by Richard Wilkinson. See also Rothstein (2008) on this topic.

4. Much of the promise of the small-school model rests on the belief that a relatively small size makes it easier for teachers to unify in purpose and practice and work together to build strong learning cultures and opportunities for students.

5. Citing federal statistics, Conley (2007) notes that 40% of students nationally need to take a remedial or developmental course upon entrance to college. Among those who take a remedial reading class, only 17% receive a bachelor's degree or higher (p. 10).

6. These percentages are based on self-reported information from a survey of UPCS graduates conducted in 2007–08, with 83% of the graduates responding. For more data on the preparation of high school students for college, see Greene and Forster (2003).

7. See in particular the report of the National Association for College Admission Counseling (2008). For additional perspective, see Conley (2007) and FairTest (2007).

8. McNeil (2000) documents the lower expectations and mental disengagement that resulted in classrooms in Texas driven by curriculum control and bureaucratic mandates. See also Darling-Hammond (1997), in particular pp. 83–93.

9. According to the Education Trust (2006), Massachusetts in 2006 was 4% below the national average of "educational effort," although its per-pupil spending level of $7,966 was above (see Table 2 in the report).

10. Personalization and small school size have received considerable attention as factors bearing on opportunity and performance, in particular during the past 15 years of high school reform. See, for example, Daniels, Bizar, and Zemelman (2001), Toch (2004), and DiMartino, Clarke, and Wolk (2003). In the UPCS example, I allude to the importance of school-family communication in the process of personalization. This topic is outside my immediate focus on internal school culture, but the two are certainly related. The power of personalization in the learning community expands to the extent that parents and students together are welcomed and brought periodically into the process of determining strategies and goals. This involvement may be a culture shift for many schools and may require concerted and creative effort, particularly when it comes to establishing communication and relationships with parents who do not speak English or who feel disconnected from the school environment for different reasons.

11. My intention in this section is to highlight key dimensions and characteristics of teaching practice in the interest of establishing a basic framework for discussion. For a comprehensive treatment, begin with recent publications sponsored by the National Research Council (2005) or Darling-Hammond and Bransford (2005).

12. For valuable perspective on the power of strong teacher learning communities to shape classroom learning, see McLaughlin and Talbert (2001). For a more general discussion on professional learning, see Lieberman and Miller (2001).

13. See also Darling-Hammond and Bransford (2005), p. 13.

14. See Elmore (2004).

Chapter 2

1. One sign of this period of social ferment is "Freeland Street" (where UPCS is located), named in honor of the Free Soil movement that received a strong impetus in Worcester, where the Free Soil Party of Massachusetts was launched in 1848.

2. The calculations are mine, based on the school population data reported by the public schools in the works cited in the text (that is, Worcester Public Schools, 1905, 1951, and 2006).

3. The reports of the Worcester Regional Research Bureau, Inc., from 2004 through 2008 are also relevant. By way of comparison, attendance at UPCS was about 95%, apparently closer to the norm in historical terms: In both 1904 and 1950, average student attendance at South High was about 94.5% (Worcester Public Schools, 1905; Worcester Public Schools, 1951).

4. These words are recorded on a dedicatory plaque in Jonas Clark Hall, Clark University, Worcester, Massachusetts.

5. UPCS graduates, spanning the legacy class of 2003 through 2007, were surveyed about their college readiness and experience as part of a project sponsored

jointly by the school and university. We are indebted to the Nellie Mae Education Foundation, in particular the Partnership for College Success program, which has spurred and supported our ongoing examination of college readiness, and also to Jonathan Starr, whose support has allowed us to work diligently with UPCS alumni.

6. According to O'Brien (2005), nationally about 31% of low income 18–24-year-olds attend college, and only 6–8% graduate within 6 years.

7. The university Web site (http://www.clarku.edu/departments/education/upcs/index.cfm) and associated links, including a link describing a training program conducted in conjunction with Boston-based Jobs for the Future, provide information on UPCS.

8. For an early assessment of the plan and challenges in implementing it, see Del Prete and Ross (2003).

9. The Advancement Via Individual Determination (AVID) program is designed to help prepare students "in the middle" for college. Information is available at the AVID Web site (http://www.avidonline.org/).

10. See, for example, Neufeld (2007).

11. My data summary draws primarily on annual reports by the Worcester Regional Research Bureau, Inc. (2003, 2004, 2005, 2006, 2007, 2008). In a few cases —for example, the number of students in advanced placement courses—I used data available from the schools. Statewide test scores (MCAS) for each Worcester school are available at each school's profile on the Web site of the Massachusetts Department of Elementary and Secondary Education. Go to http://profiles.doe.mass.edu/ (select "public school" under "Organization Type" and "Worcester" under "City Town," then choose a particular school and click on the assessment tab for that school).

Chapter 3

1. Among many possible works, I would suggest the following as starting points for delving into this literature: Moore, Alvermann, Hinchman (2000); Vacca and Vacca (2002); Fielding, Schoenbach, and Jordan (2003).

2. For a thoughtful analysis of knowledge in relation to professional practice, and distinctions among basic, applied, and reflective research, see Schon (1983, 1987). For the kind of clinical knowledge that teachers generate as they pay attention to students' interaction with subject matter, see, in particular, "Teaching as Research" in Duckworth (1996), pp. 150–168. See Darling-Hammond and Bransford (2005) for a discussion of the connection between the nonroutine nature of teaching and the importance of learning with and from colleagues, in particular, p. 13.

3. Lagemann (2002), past president of the Spencer Foundation, makes a strong and illuminating argument for generating usable knowledge in education grounded in recognition of the complex, distinctive, and contextual demands of teaching practice.

Chapter 5

1. For historical perspective, see Cuban (1984).

2. See, in particular, Stigler and Hiebert (1999), pp. 142–146.

Chapter 6

1. The idea of literature circles was developed and popularized by Daniels (2002) and other educators. For a discussion of how to adapt this collaborative learning strategy to the way of knowing of history, see Chapter 9 of this volume.

2. See Conley (2004, 2007).

Chapter 7

1. All of Chris's remarks in this chapter are taken from written reflections he made in a draft of the text, unless otherwise noted.

Chapter 8

1. See Heath (1983) and Rose (1990). Gee (2004), an educational linguist, goes a step further. He suggests that students need to do more than master the academic forms of language in a world in which multiple kinds of languages are evolving as part of the high-tech global economy.

Chapter 10

1. Based on data collected from surveys and interviews with UPCS graduates conducted in 2007–08.

References

Agee, J., & Evans, W. (1966). *Let us now praise famous men*. New York: Ballantine Books. (Original work published 1939)

Alliance for Excellent Education. (n.d.). *Understanding high school graduation rates in the United States*. Retrieved June 27, 2008, from http://www.all4ed.org/files/National_wc.pdf

Berger, N., & McLynch, J. (2006, June 20). *Public school funding in Massachusetts: Putting recent reform proposals in context*. Boston: Massachusetts Budget and Policy Center.

Berliner, D. (2006). Our impoverished view of educational reform. *Teachers College Record*, 108(6), 1–60. Retrieved January 6, 2009, from http://www.tcrecord.org/content.asp?contentid=12106

Black student college graduation rates inch higher but a large racial gap persists. (2007).*The Journal of Blacks in Higher Education*. Retrieved June 27, 2008, from http://www.jbhe.com/preview/winter07preview.html

Bruner, J. (1960). *The process of education*. Cambridge, MA: Harvard University Press.

Christensen, F., & Christensen, B. (1978). *Notes toward a new rhetoric: Nine essays for teachers* (2nd ed.). New York: Harper & Row.

Cohen, E. (1994). *Designing groupwork: Strategies for the heterogeneous classroom*. New York: Teachers College Press.

Coleman, J. S., Campbell, E., Hobson, C., McPartland, J., Mood, A., Weinfeld, F. D., & York, R. (1966). *Equality of educational opportunity study*. Washington DC: Department of Health, Education, and Welfare.

Conant, J. B. (1959). *The American high school today: A first report to interested citizens*. New York: McGraw-Hill.

Conley, D. T. (2004). *College knowledge: What it really takes for students to succeed and what we can do to get them ready*. San Francisco: Jossey-Bass.

Conley, D. T. (2007). *Toward a more comprehensive conception of college readiness*. Eugene, OR: Educational Policy Improvement Center. Available from the Center for Educational Policy Research Web site, http://cepr.uoregon.edu/

Cremin, L. A. (Ed.). (1957). *The republic and the school: Horace Mann on the education of free men*. New York: Teachers College Press.

Cuban, L. (1984). *How teachers taught: Constancy and change in American classrooms, 1890–1980*. New York: Longman.

Daniels, H. (2002). *Literature circles: Voice and choice in book clubs and reading groups* (2nd ed.). Portland, ME: Stenhouse.

Daniels, H., Bizar, M., & Zemelman, S. (2001). *Rethinking high school: Best practice in* teaching, learning, and leadership. Portsmouth, NH: Heinemann.

Darling-Hammond, L. (1997). *The right to learn: A blueprint for creating schools that work*. San Francisco: Jossey Bass.

Darling-Hammond, L., & Bransford, J. (Eds.). (2005). *Preparing teachers for a changing world: What teachers should learn and be able to do*. San Francisco: Jossey-Bass.

Del Prete, T. (1997). The rounds model of professional development. *From the Inside, 1*(1), 12–13.

Del Prete, T., & Ross, L. (2003). Blurring boundaries: The promise and challenge of a district-community action plan for systemic high school change in Worcester, MA. In K. Pittman, N. Yohalem, & J. Tolman (Eds.), *New directions in youth development: No. 97. When, where, what and how youth learn: Blurring school and community boundaries* (pp. 89–105).

Dickinson, E. (1961). "Hope" is the thing with feathers. In T. Johnson (Ed.), *Final harvest: Emily Dickinson's poems*. Boston: Little, Brown. (Original published n.d.)

DiMartino, J., Clarke, J., & Wolk, D. (Eds.). (2003). *Personalized learning: Preparing high school students to create their futures*. Lanham, MD: Scarecrow Press.

Duckworth, E. (1996). *"The having of wonderful ideas" and other essays on teaching and learning* (2nd ed.). New York: Teachers College Press.

The Education Trust. (2006). *Funding gaps 2006*. Washington, DC: Author. Retrieved April 17, 2009, from http://www2.edtrust.org/NR/rdonlyres/CDEF9403-5A75437E-93FFEBF1174181FB/0/FundingGap2006.pdf

Elmore, R. F. (2003). A plea for strong practice. *Educational Leadership, 61*(3), 6–10.

Elmore, R. F. (2004). *School reform from the inside out: Policy, practice, and performance*. Cambridge, MA: Harvard University Press.

FairTest. (2007, August 20). *SAT I: A faulty instrument for predicting college success*. Retrieved June 27, 2008, from http://www.fairtest.org/sat-i-faulty-instrument-predicting-college-success

Fielding, A., Schoenbach, R., & Jordan, M. (Eds.). (2003). *Building academic literacy: Lessons from Reading Apprenticeship classrooms, grades 6–12*. San Francisco: Jossey-Bass.

Fullan, M. (2006). *Turnaround leadership*. San Francisco: Jossey-Bass.

Gee, J. P. (2004). *Situated language and learning: A critique of traditional schooling*. New York: Routledge.

Greene, J. P., & Forster, G. (2003, September). *Public high school graduation and college readiness rates in the United States*. Education Working Paper (Manhattan Institute for Policy Research), No. 3. Retrieved April 16, 2009, from http://www.manhattan institute.org/html/ewp_03.htm

Haberman, M. (1991). The pedagogy of poverty: The pedagogy of poverty versus good teaching. *Phi Delta Kappan, 73*(4), 290–294. Retrieved April 10, 2008, from http://www.ednews.org/articles/610/1/Pedagogy-ofPoverty-The Pedagogy-of-Poverty-Versus-GoodTeaching/Page1.html

Hawkins, D. (1974). *The informed vision: Essays on learning and human nature.* New York: Agathon Press.

Heath, S. B. (1983). *Ways with words: Language, life, and work in communities and classrooms.* New York: Cambridge University Press.

Hill, P. T., Campbell, C., & Harvey, J. (2000). *It takes a city: Getting serious about urban school reform.* Washington, DC: Brookings Institution.

Hirsch, E. D. (2008, February 16). The knowledge connection. *The Washington Post,* p. A21.

Jacobowitz, R., Weinstein, M. G., Maguire, C., Luekens, M., & Fruchter, N. (2007). *The effectiveness of small high schools, 1994–95 to 2003–04.* New York: Institute for Education and Social Policy, Steinhardt School of Culture, Education, and Human Development, New York University.

Lagemann, E. C. (2002, January 24). *Usable knowledge in education: A memorandum for the Spencer Foundation board of directors.*

Lee, V. E., & Smith, J.B. (2001). *Restructuring high school for equity and excellence: What works.* New York: Teachers College Press.

Lieberman, A., & Miller, L. (Eds.). (2001). *Teachers caught in the action: Professional development that matters.* New York: Teachers College Press.

Massachusetts Department of Elementary and Secondary Education. (2000, November). *Massachusetts mathematics curriculum framework.* Malden, MA: Author. Available from the Massachusetts Department of Elementary and Secondary Education Web site, http://www.doe.mass.edu/frameworks/current.html

Massachusetts Department of Elementary and Secondary Education. (2001, June). *Massachusetts English language arts curriculum framework.* Malden, MA: Author. Available from the Massachusetts Department of Elementary and Secondary Education Web site, http://www.doe.mass.edu/frameworks/current.html

Massachusetts Department of Elementary and Secondary Education. (2003, August). *Massachusetts history and social science curriculum framework.* Malden, MA: Author. Available from the Massachusetts Department of Elementary and Secondary Education Web site, http://doe.mass.edu/frameworks/current.html.

Massachusetts Department of Elementary and Secondary Education. (2005). *Report of fact-finding review: Accelerated learning lab, Worcester public schools.* Retrieved May 22, 2008, from http://www.doe.mass.edu/sda/review/cohorts/2005/03480275fact.pdf

Massachusetts Department of Elementary and Secondary Education. (2006, October). *Massachusetts science and technology/engineering curriculum framework.* Malden, MA: Author. Available from the Massachusetts Department of Elementary and Secondary Education. Web site, http://www.doe.mass.edu/frameworks/current.html

Massachusetts Department of Elementary and Secondary Education. (2007, September 25). *MA outscores every other state on NAEP exams again.* Retrieved January 6, 2009, from http://www.doe.mass.edu/news/news.asp?id=3692

Massachusetts Department of Elementary and Secondary Education and Massachusetts Department of Higher Education. (2008, February). *Massachusetts school-to-college report: High school class of 2005.* Malden, MA: Author. Available from Massachusetts Department of Elementary and Secondary Education Web site, www.doe.mass.edu/research/reports/0208bhe.pdf

McCall, M. S., Hauser, C., Cronin, J., Kingsbury, G. G., & Houser, R. (2006, November). *Achievement gaps: An examination of differences in student achievement and growth.* Lake Oswego, OR: Northwest Evaluation Association. Retrieved January 6, 2009, from http://www.nwea.org/research/achievementgap.asp?ref=direct

McLaughlin, M. W., & Talbert, J. E. (2001). *Professional communities and the work of high school teaching.* Chicago: University of Chicago Press.

McNeil, L. M. (2000). *Contradictions of school reform: Educational costs of standardized testing.* New York: Routledge.

Merton, T. (1979). *Love and living* (N. B. Stone & P. Hart, Eds.). New York: Harcourt Brace. (Original work published 1967)

Moore, D., Alvermann, D. E., & Hinchman, K. A. (Eds.). (2000). *Struggling adolescent readers: A collection of teaching strategies.* Newark, DE: International Reading Association.

National Association for College Admission Counseling. (2008, September). Report of the commission on the use of standardized tests in undergraduate admission. Arlington, VA: Author. Retrieved January 6, 2009, from http://www.nacacnet.org/PublicationsResources/Research/Documents/Testing Comission_FinalReport.pdf

National Commission on Teaching and America's Future. (1996). *What matters most: Teaching for America's future.* New York: Author.

National Commission on Teaching and America's Future. (2003). *No dream denied: A pledge to America's children.* Washington, DC: Author.

National Council of Teachers of Mathematics. (n.d.). *Barbie Bungee.* Retrieved January 7, 2009, from http://illuminations.nctm.org/LessonDetail.aspx?ID=L646

National Research Council. Committee on How People Learn, A Targeted Report for Teachers. (2005). *How students learn: History, mathematics, and science in the classroom.* Washington, DC: National Academies Press.

Neufeld, B. (2007). Instructional improvement in the Boston Public Schools: The limits of focus and stability. In S. P. Reville & C. Coggins (Eds.), *A decade of urban school reform: Persistence and progress in the Boston Public Schools* (pp. 133–151). Cambridge, MA: Harvard Education Press.

O'Brien, C. (2005). *Indicators of opportunity in higher education: 2005 status report.* Washington, DC: The Pell Institute for the Study of Opportunity in Higher Education. Available from the Pell Institute Web site, http://www.pellinstitute.org/files/6_Indicators.pdf

Orfield, G., & Lee, C. (2005). *Why segregation matters: Poverty and educational inequality.* Cambridge, MA: Civil Rights Project, Harvard University. Available from the Pell Institute Web site, http://www.civilrightsproject.ucla.edu/research/deseg/Why_Segreg_Matters.pdf

Patrick Administration Education Action Agenda. (2008, June). *Ready for 21st century success: The new promise of public education.* Boston: Massachusetts Executive Office of Education. Available from the Massachusetts government Web site, http://www.mass.gov/Agov3/docs/Readiness%20Final%20Report.pdf

Perkins, G. (Ed.). (1972). *American poetic theory.* New York: Holt, Rinehart & Winston.

Perrone, V. (1991). *A letter to teachers: Reflections on schooling and the art of teaching.* San Francisco: Jossey Bass.

Rose, M. (1990). *Lives on the boundary.* New York: Penguin Books.

Rothstein, R. (2004). *Class and schools: Using social, economic, and educational reform to close the black-white achievement gap.* Washington, DC: Economic Policy Institute; New York: Teachers College Press.

Rothstein, R. (2008). Whose problem is poverty? *Educational Leadership, 65*(7), 8–13.

Saint-Exupéry, A. de (1971). *The little prince* (K. Woods, Trans.). New York: Harcourt Brace Jovanovich. (Original work published 1943)

Schön, D. (1983). *The reflective practitioner: How professionals think in action.* New York: Basic Books.

Schön, D. (1987). *Educating the reflective practitioner.* San Francisco, CA: Jossey-Bass.

Shulman, L. (1986). Those who understand: Knowledge growth in teaching. *Educational Researcher, 15*(2), 4–14.

Stigler, J. W., & Hiebert, J. (1999). *The teaching gap: Best ideas from the world's teachers for improving education in the classroom.* New York: Free Press.

Surrette, K. (2007). [Reflection paper for Education 152]. Unpublished manuscript, Clark University, Worcester, MA.

Thoreau, H. D. (1996). *Walden.* Cologne, Germany: Konemann. (Original work published 1854)

Toch, T. (2004). *High schools on a human scale: How small schools can transform American education.* Boston: Beacon Press.

U.S. Department of Education. (2006). *Answering the challenge of a changing world: Strengthening education for the 21st century.* Available: http://www.ed.gov/teachers/how/prep/higher/competitiveness.html

Vacca, R. T. & Vacca, J. L. (2002). *Content area reading: Literacy and learning across the curriculum* (7th ed.). Boston: Allyn & Bacon.

Wilkinson, R. (2005). *The impact of inequality: How to make sick societies healthier.* New York: New Press.

Wineburg, S. (2001). *Historical thinking and other unnatural acts: Charting the future of teaching the past.* Philadelphia: Temple University Press.

Worcester Public Schools. (1905). *Report of the public schools of the city of Worcester, 1904.* Worcester, MA: The Hamilton Press.

Worcester Public Schools. (1951). *Annual report of the superintendent of public schools of the city of Worcester for the year ending December 31, 1950.* Worcester, MA: Author.

Worcester Public Schools. (2006). *October 1 report.* Worcester, MA: Author.

Worcester Public Schools. (2007). *October 1 report.* Worcester, MA: Author.

Worcester Regional Research Bureau, Inc. (2001). *The 2000 census: A preliminary look at Worcester and the region* (Report no. 01-05). Worcester, MA: Author.

Worcester Regional Research Bureau, Inc. (2003). *Benchmarking public education in Worcester: 2003.* Worcester, MA: Author.

Worcester Regional Research Bureau, Inc. (2004). *Benchmarking public education in Worcester: 2004.* Worcester, MA: Author.

Worcester Regional Research Bureau, Inc. (2005). *Benchmarking public education in Worcester: 2005*. Worcester, MA: Author.

Worcester Regional Research Bureau, Inc. (2006). *Benchmarking public education in Worcester: 2006*. Worcester, Massachusetts: Author.

Worcester Regional Research Bureau, Inc. (2007). *Benchmarking public education in Worcester: 2007*. Worcester, Massachusetts: Author.

Worcester Regional Research Bureau, Inc. (2008). *Benchmarking public education in Worcester: 2008*. Worcester, Massachusetts: Author.

Index

About the Author

Thomas Del Prete is Director of the Jacob Hiatt Center for Urban Education and Chair of the Education Department at Clark University in Worcester, Massachusetts. He has worked for more than two decades on teacher education, university-school partnership, and school reform.